Solidarity Forever? The Struggle of an Occupier

I0426226

By Al R. Suarez

Table of contents

1
Introduction

The image with my intro is of my first occupy protest with my favorite sign, which my friends in Georgia still have. First let me explain the cover image of this book. Part of the title covered my mouth and at first that was unintentional. However it also symbols how I have been silenced as an activist, and this book is my mouth speaking to the masses. Also accept my apologies for the format, not all the page numbers are in the far corner and page 34 is not on page 34. This is an account of my 11 months of struggle in the occupy movement (September-2011-August 2012) where I stayed on camps throughout the east coast (Burlington, VT, Boston, MA, Providence, RD, New Haven, CT, Washington, DC, Tampa, FL) some of the best, and some of the worst, moments of my life happened in this movement, an emotional and spiritual roller-coaster. The life of an occupier is fast, I had to decide between wearing a mask or showing my face, and I showed my face. In each occupy there were different people, for example Harvard people are far less conservative than Yale people. I lived abroad for some years and I became more than an activist but a revolutionary when coming back giving me a different perspective. Occupy was an opportunity to do things I would not have been able to do otherwise. Like being able to call Supreme Justice Scalia a traitor to his face at Weslyan University.

I never considered myself paranoid but many activists are and give nom-de-plume or nom-de-guerre depending on their actions, like who is mentioned later "Ping Pong" or "Big Red" or "Little Red" names that are used with affection, among their comrades, or at least those they think are, those who are not, are not given a name at all. We always had to deal with people driving by, whether students or not, yelling at our camp, get a job! It came with the territory, literally. I was arrested two times defending occupy which is described here, like many activists I became one as a teenager soon after 911, having been interested in politics before that, but being an activist as of 12 years ago, believing in peaceful revolution, in the end the pen is mightier than the sword. Some parts of this story are blocked out of my mind from the trauma, and certain details and people are not mentioned in respect for their privacy, but most of the events I recollect from those months will be described for the purpose of history, as a vindication as well, for my efforts in the movement, which were unfortunately mostly not reciprocated by other members of the movement in-spite of all their chants of "solidarity".

Numbers at the General Assemblies have diminished, at Occupy Boston where we used to have over 2000 people now only about 10 show up to the latest meetings. This account shows how we were demoralized from within and what can be done to revive the movement. The movement initially was all

2

inclusive but out of a reaction to being too inclusive it has become too exclusive, there needs to be a balance. Articles within the movement were published describing the tactics used to divide our movement, just as what happened to me, but even that was not sufficient for vindication. From the cold to the heat I stayed on camps, I shall not forget. The story starts in Georgia, then Vermont, but it should really start in my hometown, Boston, when Richard Knight drove me to my Nana's house, and I prayed at the grave of my grandfather, promising to be a good grandson, and a good uncle to my niece, as I continued in my struggle, in my travels.

The camps or collectives (occupy) were like the kibbutzim in Palestine, communities of sharing and equality, an oasis in a desert of injustice. At least it was that way in the beginning. I encountered activists with a tradition of fighting for freedom in their family, some going back very far, like a descendant of Robert de Bruce, the King of Scotland after the death of William Wallace (Bruce Wright). Others were black sheeps, people who escaped their affluent family and joined the poor in their struggle in the ultimate act of solidarity. At times we felt like outcasts of society, the forgotten, the voiceless, who were finally given a voice. I encountered veterans, like those I marched with as an honorary member in NYC, or like in DC, veterans who were natural leaders, and received a sir yes sir depending on their rank from other soldiers in occupy, people who hitchhiked bravely from Boston to DC while we took buses, many were members of Veterans for Peace. People who were loyal, would keep an eye on my back-pack or get it out of harm's way. Back when you did not have to worry about getting robbed on camp or locking your tent.

It is necessary in this intro to thank a few people for without their help I would not be here today writing this book. Ty & Sarah Hailey, who took me in their home in a time of need in New Haven, as well as Racheal & Shara Rabich, who took me in their home near Savannah and helped me out in a time of need. Lastly, my father, who is with me now, when I am starting this book, on the anniversary of my sister's passing, who did what he could during my struggle.

Dedicated to my late sister Natasha Suarez, and my niece, her daughter, Mercedes, so she can have an account of what her uncle went through the months after her mother passed, for when she gets older, the activism I did for her future.

Chapter 1 Tragedy

Occupy started in New York in mid-September 2011, however it is necessary as I was an activist far before my sister's death, to give the account of her death and the immediate aftermath of that, which can help you better understand my situation by the time occupy came around. My sister died suddenly on September 2nd 2011, she was just a couple days in the hospital, I was due to fly into Burlington, VT the day after she died, I was able to see her body but refused, she would not want me to see her that

3

way, the funeral was with a closed casket. Rather to delve into how she died and the mysterious circumstances around it, I will just say her death came as a shock to us all, leaving behind her three year old daughter. Soon after her death while I was living with my mother in Statesboro, GA I went down to visit fellow activists in Florida, this was just before occupy was to start, then when I came back to Georgia I heard there was a occupy protest planned in Savannah from an event on Facebook. I immediately left a comment on the event asking if anyone could give me a ride. This is how I first got into contact with Racheal. She, her two kids, and Shara, gave me a ride to my first occupy protest, it was quite an experience.

There was never to be a camp, the nearest one was in Atlanta, but it was still quite a protest, with a few dozen comrades, all anti-system but with different views, this movement which by October, had spread through-out the nation, was still in its very beginning. There is like in Tampa, in Savannah a homeless population of well over 10,000 people, in the beginning helping the homeless was a major part of the movement. I made a sign with my favorite chant, still is, in English and Spanish "El Pueblo Unido Jamas Sera Vencido/The People United Will Never Be Defeated". It seems so ironic to me now with the division the movement has suffered lately.

On the evening of October 12th tensions with my mother heightened, by then I already had comrades who came from Florida to be one of the first to Occupy DC, and I wanted to leave Georgia. In fact when I left Georgia I ran into someone on the bus who had already been to Occupy DC and met my comrade Bruce. However, I ended up getting kicked out and homeless in order to leave, Racheal helped me with a motel and my father and his family sent me money to take a bus, finding my way back to Vermont to see my niece. On the long bus trip there God gave me a vision of my father in the future reunited with my niece, and this gave me the will to live, leaving all suicidal thoughts from my mind, much of my sadness turned to anger at the injustice my family suffered. This vision was much long the character James Franco plays in 127 hours of his future son that gave him the will to live. It's funny since later in Vermont I met an activist who looks like James Franco. I ended up to my first occupy camp in Burlington, where tragedy was soon to strike, something that was becoming quite familiar to me. Only three weeks into occupy a member of our camp apparently shot himself, and so the next chapter will describe this experience.

Chapter 2 Vermont

I arrived in the park in Burlington with almost all my things ready to find a tent and spent the night on camp, I believe the date was November 1st 2011, and I happened to have left the country to Spain on November 1st 2006, I had previously been staying with a "friend" of my late sister near Middlebury. I came wearing my white and black hat, that looks like a gulf hat, it was the hat I wore with my sister on our last summer and in all my travels I still have it in my possession as it holds great sentimental value.

4

Like my sister, I went to high school in Middlebury, and went to my first major protest in Burlington, against the war in Afghanistan at the age of 17 in October 2001, we were exposing the pipeline plans, I was in the local paper for this and was almost arrested. My sister was not interested in politics at the time, my Mom encouraged my interest. I was lucky to get back to Burlington, I found a cheap bus that would take me from Middlebury to Burlington, about an hour trip, as I had been meaning to check out this camp since when I arrived in Vermont, about October 15th. There was a logistics tent where I asked a woman, who looked to be in her late 30s, heavy set, her names escapes me, who worked with the safety group (like security on camp), directed me to a man who was to find an available tent for me. I believe he was one of the homeless occupiers on camp and knew the area well. The camp had been going on just about a week, if I had gone there on the 15th there would not have been any tents yet, but much happened in my 3 week stay there.

I presented myself as a freelance journalist, and with my netbook & cell phone was able to do an interview from camp on my online radio show, but eventually it became clear to the occupiers I was also an activist and I wanted to take part in their movement, as many freelancers had ended up doing, people like Tyler Westbrook who I had long been acquainted with from Facebook from his activism in the Middle East, I knew he was a native of Vermont, and I did not recognize him at first or realize he was on camp. By then I had 1000s of contacts on Facebook, activists through-out the nation, many having ended up joining the ranks of occupy, people I ended up running into or knew were on location. Tyler and I ended up working the safety group overnight on camp and would make sure belligerents coming from the clubs at night or homeless invaders would not disturb camp, Tyler was more compassionate than I, and would even offer a tent to a stranger that night to sleep in rather than confront them. Many times I witnessed in order to "deescalate" the confrontation actually made the situation worse, as we were not equipped to deal with such matters, the same problems arose on all the camps I stayed on. How we dealt with belligerents came back to haunt us when an apparent suicide happened on camp.

The tent I was given the first day I had difficulty closing, and it was cold, when I did finally zipper it up I was stuck inside not being able to open it up, finally someone helped me open it, but it was damaged. Later I saw a drunk homeless man sleep in it, luckily I was able to get my things out. I ended up sleeping with a couple comrades in the logistics tent, one of whom was intoxicated. The two sobers were Tyler and I, Tyler was only to sleep a short while as he was to work safety that night, he was a devoted occupier. That night I heard him talk about Palestine, then suddenly I knew why he was familiar, I had seen his documentary in Gaza, we had written each other on Facebook, from that moment Tyler and I formed a bond on camp, and our bond would not break even when all the drama against me from occupy was happening and we had heated words on a Facebook group.

Tyler used to like to wear the kaffiyeh, the Arab scarf, even during press conferences, and he often brought his camera to film our marches, his daughter Khalila I believe her name is, a Arab name, a young woman in her late 20s I believe, also came to camp with him from time to time. He told us stories of his trips, and had long conversations with him into the night. Anyway when Tyler got up to do safety that night in the logistics tent, I stayed awake, and suddenly the drunk man pulled out his penis and started peeing right there at the entrance of the logistics tent in front of everyone. I later joked luckily we did not have a woman come by asking about occupy at that moment, she would get the wrong impression. I was pissed, literally, even making the joke I was angry, so I asked for another tent.

5

Lucking the ISO comrades (International Socialist Organization) had a big red tent that only had one or two people in it, so I slept there, the logistics tent had sleeping bags, blankets, etc, they provided I used.

I don't remember if it was my second or third night there but I had my first of 2 sexual experiences on a occupy camp with a woman who needed a tent to sleep in who I was hanging out with earlier in the day, there was another couple in the big red tent, who were making out, by the time I let her in they were passed out. I slept by myself but she asked me to come closer to her, I started to rest and she woke me up by laughing, it was clear what she wanted, I had some wine in me, which was the norm on camp to make you feel warm (as long as you drank inside your tent you were alright) and she had some in her too, so I kissed her to stop her laughing, one thing led to another, she had a condom, and had left the tent by early morning, out of respect for her privacy I won't mention who she is but she was just a "traveler" or "weekender" someone who was there to party not to do activism. I found out later a guy had kicked her out of his tent earlier that night having rejected her. I won't say more a gentleman would not do that.

A man who's name escapes me, but was known as a jerk on camp, but who I had sympathy with, brought the "Teepee Community Center" to the right side of camp. Few people took part in building it, but in the end I was the only one fighting to take its contents off camp before the cops could destroy it after our camp was shut down. This man let me stay with him a night when most people stayed at the church and he ended up driving me to Boston, they had the Socialist Labor Forum or whatever it was called, at Harvard, we did not make it but we spent a night at Occupy Boston.

A man's whose name I do remember who went to Boston with the ISO people as I missed that ride, Richard Knight, was to be an ally of mine and meet me at many occupies from New York to Tampa, a man in his early 30s from a upper middle class background in Texas, decided to take a road-trip all the way to Vermont to be with occupy. I would have went with him to Montreal, and miss the raid on the camp in Burlington but my passport was elsewhere, I was there that night for a reason. Richard heard from Occupy Montreal about the suicide and the raid, and came down around the time we were converging on the church. Richard had driven me to Middlebury to try to get my remaining things, where we spent the night at Roxanna Emilo's house, her son was a friend of my sister. It is interesting to note a third man who took the trip to Boston with me I ran into at a church in NYC where occupiers used to stay, he was literally the first man I saw when I walked in the door, I told him of how I was arrested with Occupy Boston. Unfortunately, one of my weaknesses is names, I am a faces person, and unless someone has got close to me I rarely remember their name.

I will now attempt to give my account of the "suicide" and the raid. I arrived on camp to police taping off a section of it and occupiers crying and hugging everywhere, I had no idea what happened, an officer told me there was a shooting. I later found out someone named Josh Pfenning, who they say was a soldier, apparently shot them-self in their tent with two others present, they had been drinking, and they were drunk, the cops were questioning the two other guys. I knew who one of the two guys was, he was a trouble maker and there has been an attempt to kick him off camp before. I did not know who the guy who got shot was till after he died. Rumors of foul play started circling almost immediately after the shooting. Paparazzi type journalists started taking photos of us grieving, as we could feel the

6

imminent destruction of our camp, it was not just about the guy who was shot, I told the press to back off, and they did, at least while I was there, a anger was growing inside me.

First Tasha, now Josh, there was to be two other deaths in occupy I was to go through, one of which I attended a vigil and met the family of the deceased, the Arredando family, the deceased was the brother of a veteran who died in Iraq, him and his father started Camp Alex named after the first son, which also happens to be my name, I believe the son who killed himself was the same age as me, they were supporters of occupy, as they lived near me in Boston (Jamaica Plain), and many common friends knew them, it was during one of my brief pauses of homelessness, but I will get into that later.
There was a GA (General Assembly) the night of the shooting, the same place where we had a concert with Gogol Bordello the night before, a gypsy punk band. Everyone spoke of the importance of keeping the camp, this is more or less what I said: "Now is the test of whether you are a occupier or not, we must converge on the Teepee, we still have a camp!" People took my advice and started meeting by the Teepee after we got word that the man who was shot was pronounced dead. I went inside the Teepee and there was much tension, especially between the kid who was just released by police who was in the tent when Josh shot himself, and the guy who started the Teepee, Tyler was there, and he was crying, it was hard seeing such a strong man cry, I was still in shock. Then we got word the city invited us into the near-by City Hall, I had a feeling it was a set-up, someone told me to bring my back pack with my computer in case we were raided, but I said I would come back for it.

As we met with the Mayor and the Chief of Police Tyler got a text that they were taking over the rest of the encampment, it was a set up indeed, we all ran out and saw cops with tear gas canisters ready to detain and shoot us. Hailey was briefly detained, and everyone was yelling at the cops to let her go, the "hero" mayor eventually ordered the cops to let her go. I was back at the Teepee that had not been taken over yet, and my back pack was gone, later that night at the church someone told me it was there waiting for me, my computer was still inside it, with images of my sister, dear to me, that would be the first of two times I lost it and found it again. None of the local media wanted to publish anything on how the Teepee was destroyed.

Before we headed to Boston we asked comrades to make sure the cops would not throw out its remains, but nothing was done with all the confusion. On the way to Boston the guy who brought us went on about using the word "renaissance" instead of revolution, and talking to the 1 percent at Harvard to help us, I said the idea was bourgeois and he took it as a joke, but I meant it. The Boston occupiers like in Vermont did not like him, in fact called him a cop to his face, as they smiled at me, this pissed him off. No one ever called me a cop then. I guess I had a likable face. My great uncle was actually a cop who gave his life for the city of Boston, cops are workers, with pensions, part of the 99% and although they were used against us are not necessarily the enemy.

The same day we came back to Vermont after our short trip, I attempted to move the remains of the community center but cops stopped me, just a few things got out which a comrade with his truck helped me take out to an elderly woman's house, a local supporter, named Jay Vos, where I stayed a couple nights. A German man in his late 40s named Gerhard I believe, was helping a homeless woman friend of mine who had problems with the cops and drinking, was depressed about Josh, and I ended up staying in a tent in his backyard with her, and then he offered me his room for a few days before I moved to Occupy Boston.

7

By then I knew how to handle the media, to use talking points, and the rest is irrelevant. For after the shooting on camp when Josh was dying local Fox News asked people if they thought the weather was good, those that answered yes, were shown on TV saying yes to knowing there was a gun on camp, typical misinformation. Tyler called Fox and said they better do another report if they did not want us to occupy their offices, and they came and did another one, but I was too mad to give my name. I also realized the symbolism of a tent, even after we were shut down in Boston when we got out of jail at the Boston Commons we made a tent and threw it to the crowd. I also learned how to handle myself in General Assembly, the gestures and terms, although I did not like it very much, my first GA in NY they "tabled" which means it was left over from discussion from the last meeting, whether or not sexual acts were permitted in the churches where they slept, this meeting was in a church and conducted my first morning in NY after spending the night there, as I arrived the night before New Years Eve, was hectic, they were later kicked out of the churches. I will finish this chapter with what I wrote soon after the camp in Burlington was shut down.

Revival of Occupy Burlington

By Al Suarez on Friday, November 18, 2011 at 6:53am ·

It is still very painful for me to delve into the tragedy at Occupy Burlington, I rather at this time focus on the positive, on the events that unfolded last night that were truly inspiring. Yesterday at about 5pm at City Park, several dozen of us set up a "free speech zone". A orange gate, we had encircled ourselves with, and led the march, followed by others with signs and what not, the homeless and with home alike, student and worker alike, all marching as equals, under the same banner of justice, of a just cause that cannot be silenced or wiped out, no matter how the city and the State come at us, our chants, from LA to New York, from Egypt to Spain, will be heard the world over.

We marched down Church St. to the surprise of many people, who have been hearing in the media our movement is dead, it is far from it. A man tried to break out free speech zone but we immediately re-assemble it, and kept marching, no one could stop us. Finally we reached the Post Office and sang solidarity with the union there against the cuts of the workers there. Then we headed down the road blocking traffic, to Edmonds Middle School, where Senator Palino, union leaders, students, and others were to meet together into the night.

Only 3 months ago in the Burlington where my sister worked and died, I spoke with her here about the new society I wanted, and we dreamed together of that new society, a better world for my niece. Off in the distance as I marched, suddenly I could see my sister's face, and I lit up, and could feel the energy of resurrection, of revival, all around us, and all the blisters in my feet, all the tiredness, went away, and all I could feel was energy, which is hard to explain, a revolutionary energy that charged us into our destiny, as we continued to defy the unjust system where the poor are left to die in the street. A wave of people came to reinforce us, old faces I could see, survivors of the storm, the storm troopers that stormed our camp in a most despicable manner, but we continue, unabated, unintimidated, till final victory, so that no more Natashas may die from this unjust system, so that my sister may live in me...

8

Chapter 3 Back To My Hometown

I arrived at the end of November one evening again at Occupy Boston this time with all my things ready to sleep in any tent available, coming alone on a bus, I was fed up with the drama of Vermont, here was a major camp in New England still alive and kicking, and in my sister and mine's hometown. I was impressed with my last trip there, did not want to go back to Vermont, so here I was to stay, at least until the camp was raided. It was the second largest occupy in the nation after New York, third was LA I believe, Boston had 100s of campers and thousands of supporters from all over New England who came to visit her, especially on the weekends where many people came to visit was to be my home, the spiritual tent, on Gandhi Way by the Gandhi statue.

I was almost immediately interviewed by John Dwyer, a distant cousin of the Kennedys, we did an interview you can find on Youtube. I had slept with him in the library tent in the early morning hours after he worked safety, it was a military tent and relatively warm, I liked being surrounded by books. He wore a Russian hat, and signaled where my comrades from Vermont were when I was looking for them the first time around, I eventually got a Russian hat as well, and John was like my Tyler on camp, he was in his late 30s, about Tyler's age, also a freelancer, but we had a fallout, as I would have with several people, although there has been some reconciliations, the drama that happened in Boston was far greater than in Vermont.

It is interesting to note there was a "mountain man" who showed me what tent I could stay in, in Boston, a redheaded man with a beard in his twenties from Vermont, there was later allegations made against him similar to mine ironically. In fact as soon as I showed up I saw Elizabeth again, the medic I had met on my prior trip, she goes by Eli Holmes now in New York, and she was in his face talking about sexual harassment, Anna Aizman from safety, who later also turned into my enemy, told me to not take up her offer to shadow her on safety, that she was crazy, I later learned she was known to accuse many of the men of harassing her or others but she never did me while I was on camp, even when I accompanied her and a few others on a trip to Occupy DC where she made a "occulover" or whatever she called the various men she dated from the camps.

So I was to stay in the spiritual tent, where I made friends with a Indian man who started the spiritual tent, his name evades me, but I will always remember the advice on anger he gave me, that anger is a good thing, that whoever tells me otherwise does not know what they are talking about, that I can channel my anger, towards something productive, that is at least what I concluded from what he told me. He was probably in his 50s with a grey beard and glasses. I also ran into Stephanie Fail, I had practiced Spanish with her briefly on my first trip, after I saw David Lumoso speak as he always did at the GA about Ocupemos el barrio which I was later to join being brought by Brian Kwoba, Brian is an Afro American man who also speaks Spanish, who I was delighted to learn was of the same ideology as me (Trotskyist). Ocupemos was a pro-immigrant group that affiliated with occupy out of East Boston (where my maternal grandparents are from) and Jamaica Plain (where I lived when I was a boy). It was started by Stanley Rosario a Dominican man, and Hector, a Puerto Rican student, along with David Lumoso who is half Puerto Rican half Cuban.

9

Stephanie's mother is an Italian Venezuelan, hence her Latin roots. She studies at UMASS where my parents went, her and Jason, who helped start Occupy UMASS, both of whom were arrested with me, Jason, a veteran, Brian and Brian's girlfriend were all arrested for the movement, and we all stayed together in Jamaica Plain after the raid on our camp. I had stayed in Stephanie's "gert" which is like a Alaskan tent, which was by the media tent, as she was part of media as well, after I left the spiritual tent which was taken over by a belligerent that night, who had an altercation later on with Dwyer, there was unfortunately no room in the gert for Dwyer, but he found another tent later that night.

One day when I was coming out of the media tent I saw standing before me one of my heroes, Norman Finkelstein. Son of holocaust survivors he has been un-intimidated confronting the Zionists and their injustice towards the Palestinians, even losing his job as a professor as a result of it. I got to tell him how I translated his Russia Today interview into Spanish subtitles after the raid on the flotilla to Gaza, I even got to ask him a question about Gandhi when he was speaking to Occupy Boston. I missed my chance to see Chomsky speak, but I met him later at his office after sneaking into Occupy Harvard, was quite a trip to Cambridge, had not been there since I was a kid and my father was studying at Harvard, as I had missed my chance the first time around to go to Harvard at the forum, Dwyer said he had a tent at Harvard Yard but was never able to go to Harvard with him.

Chapter 4 Trip to the Capitol & Back

Finally in early December I got my chance to go to Occupy DC, by then Reverend Bruce Wright, a comrade of mine, had gone back to Saint Petersburg, Florida, and was supporting Occupy Tampa, so I could not meet up with him, but in DC remained two camps, and the union financed our trip for the National General Assembly there where we had occupy delegates from 50 states, even a member from Occupy Hawaii, I filmed part of the National GA in front of the Washington Monument. However, there was suspicion between the unions and the occupiers at these events, some of the occupiers were convinced the "co-opting Democrats" of the unions paid them to go there to leave their camps defenseless, and this showed somewhat true as Occupy Philadelphia fell soon after the assembly happened, as well as other cities, and Boston was under threat, cutting our trip short. The notion was use the unions but don't let them use you. For example the union invaded Senator Scott Brown's office, I suggested we go see John Kerry since Brown was not there, and they said no, so I went there by myself and Kerry was unable to see me either.

On the bus I met someone who was kicked off of Dewey Square at Occupy Boston by the cops who I was later to meet up with in Providence, a young woman who went by the name "Ping Pong", a short, slender woman who liked to have her hair pink and short, sort of a tomboy. We were the vanguard of the camp and felt guilty for leaving, and went back on the first bus, some going back on plane, most were back by December 10th, as that morning is when the raid took place.

While I was at the YMCA taking a shower I accidentally left my cell, I ended up getting a ride back and a gentleman in his 50s, a Mexican American, drove me back in a van accompanied by another man

10

about his age, he told me he knew Cesar Chavez, was from California, and had also met Bobby Kennedy, it was a shame I could not meet him again. I planned to get arrested in DC, after the injustice in Vermont, I was convinced I was to be arrested doing civil disobedience in DC or Boston. However, logistics, and the weather, much like in Tampa later, prevented me from getting this wish. You see a lot of people don't understand this, the need to get arrested, civil disobedience is when you deliberately break a law because you want it changed, for it is unjust, it is to me, the ultimate act of patriotism, being ready to sacrifice your criminal record for a cause greater than yourself, whether defending your camp or a position, trespassing I feel is a charge that is unjust, the arrests are unjust and excessive as 1000s of occupiers have been arrested over the months.

I missed my chance to get arrested with my other comrades on K Street where the lobbyists are centered, they laid down in the rain and all got thrown in the patty wagon. I went that night to the Supreme Court in the rain to get arrested, but no one was there, no one would have known till much later I was arrested, it was supposed to be a meet up but people were already arrested or stuck in the rain. Rather than go into a tent again, where I had a rat wake me up one night, as DC is known to be full of rats, I called from SEIU people who got me a hotel room with them in Maryland I believe, on the border with DC, luckily I had some money left they had given me for a taxi, I hated going indoors, you see occupying was a way for me to punish myself for not being a good enough brother to my sister, it was all symbolic, the whole ordeal has made me stronger, although it is still traumatic for me to speak about it.

Occupiers tended to call the union people "bourgeois" or the modern term, "budgy" and prided themselves on their struggle, and I was of that same thinking. The camps were a public way to draw attention to the injustice of the homeless and the poor in the country, a problem that could no longer be ignored, but the movement needs to adapt as repression and infiltration, which I will get to later, has caused much damage to the movement, especially resulting in internal tensions and even all out civil war on the remaining camps.

So the next day, after about 3 days we were in DC, we got the word Mayor Menino of Boston was threatening to shut our camp down, and 1 of the three buses that headed out from Boston with the union was offered, but only for Occupy Boston people so some comrades stayed behind to bring occupiers from other cities to help save our camp, as Philly had already been shut down. We arrived at about 2am to see Dewey Square in Boston full of 1000s of supporters, it was very emotional, we did not know if the camp was still there, it was December 9th, that night there was only two arrests I know about, Brian and his girlfriend, they refused to move their tent from the road, they were thrown into the patty wagon kissing, very romantic, I found out these comrades were my roommates later when I moved in with Jason.

That night I saw Stephanie, who I had cried to on the phone for not coming back sooner, she gave me a big hug and ran around in circles of joy that her comrades made it back in time from DC. I gave my bags to a guy later, I did not want my things sent to the trash, I was ready to be arrested, the next day he brought the stuff back, he was one of the SEIU people who came back with us, so I met with my Nana in the South Shore as I still have family in Boston, and gave her my bags, in the early morning hours of December 10th I made the last stand, 46 of us were arrested defending Occupy Boston, it was the saddest and greatest moment of my life, I had written an article soon after about the event I will share.

11

Chapter 5 The Last Stand

"The Last Stance At Dewey-The Greatest Experience of My Life

By Al Suarez on Wednesday, December 14, 2011 at 1:05pm ·

This is my first time writing a bit at length about the event that occurred on the morning of December 10th 2011. Few moments in my life I can imagine in the future would equal our last stance that Saturday morning, getting married, having children, having my niece back in my arms, you see this stance was bigger than ourselves. For legal purposes I cannot enclose in this note the details of how we were arrested, most of you by now should know the story, I will simply attempt to describe what it meant to me, and to all of us, who were the last to leave the camp from the longest lasting occupation in the nation, and what a honor it was for me to take part in this in my hometown of Boston, after experiencing camps in Burlington, Vermont, and Washington, DC, seeing similarities, but also the exceptional dignity of those who stayed in the camp in the cold at Dewey, for a cause that is greater than our little community. But for the future of this country as I said in a mic check shortly before the boot of one of the black clothed cops was on me to take me in the "patty wagon" with my other comrades, we were the 46, of whom 13 I believe were women, including 3 personal friends of mine.

These are the toughest women I ever seen, not girls, women, in the true sense of the word, including Rita, Stephanie, and Ashley, I need not expose their last names, but they earned respect of the camp before this, and now have the respect of all the true occupiers.

After staying up late, I finally took a nap with my new tent-mate Branden, in the "Pit of Freaks", which usually was full of blankets and Anarchists, but just had him and me, Branden was one of my comrades in DC who rushed back in the first bus to Boston when we heard the news of the order of the Mayor of Boston against our camp. He left behind a friend who was imprisoned at the Supreme Court who we later found out was released. It pained him to have to leave, but I told him 'If he was not in jail he would be here with us, go for him!'. Branden is the bravest 20 year old I know. An Anarchist in the best sense of the word, and proved his manhood to us all, my voice from being in the rain in the protests at
DC was almost gone, so he spoke for me at the GA Friday night, I mean he said what I felt, what real revolutionaries or activists are willing to do, as we arrived the night before to see 1000s of supporters by the camp, only to see the next night only a few dozen left. He said he would be on the front-lines and defend the camp till the end, which is exactly what he did, I felt weak, but suddenly an urge hit me and I stood up and hugged him after he spoke. It was a honor to sleep beside him that night. It is such

12

an injustice how he has been treated since then, harassed by police left and right, but he continues to defy, and I will support him 100%.

I woke him as I heard the calls, this time which sounded for real, to wake up, the cops were there, it was about 5am. He went his way, I went mine, later I found out there was a bulldozer on the other side of the camp, and even snipers, I was on the side of the camp where there was at least 200 black clothed officers converging to take out a small stance and into the wagons that waited for us. We were offered to be arrested in front of cameras, or to be able to leave, but we mic checked that this was not a publicity stunt, we held on to the end, I gave a shout out to Vermont, this time I was ready to be arrested, and I said to my comrades to their ears, those beside me, something too special for a mic check, what a honor it was to go down with these brothers, we sang all morning in the jail Solidarity Forever, even the cops had some respect for us, we were peaceful, on public land, and nothing or no one could intimidate us.

In court yesterday too, I refused the humiliating deal of probation without going to Dewey Square a year, which was our home, out of the 25 arraigned I was of the 8 who refused, including Stephanie, such a brave woman. We will use the court as a platform to advance our cause, a cause of justice, as I told the journalists, even the "conservatives" have some respect for us, and this last stance of defiance, something tells me this is just the beginning, we came from all walks of life, workers, students, veterans, the unemployed and homeless, all together with one voice, which will never be silenced..."
It was the greatest experience indeed, there was little violence from the cops, this was because of public pressure after seeing brutality in NY and other places, the only violence happened is when Noah went limp and a cop was rough with his wrist, when I proceeded to yell "he's a peaceful protester!" the cop let up, as Noah was yelling in pain. Noah has red fuzzy hair and a beard, in his twenties, it's funny since he is half Irish half Jewish like my mother. I remember I came to the part of camp near where we used to have General Assembly and saw about 20 comrades sitting down, I saw Stephanie, as she was part of media team, I told her to cover us, but she ended up doing civil disobedience with us. I sat down in the middle in the front part, and said, lets lock arms, prayed, and it was done. I was also one of the few occupiers to not take the deal in court, we locked arms not budging, 20 of us on that side of camp,

and along with the people from the October raid on Occupy Boston from another camp, we all went to court, and are still fighting it in court as I write these words, among those still fighting that I can recollect are Jason, Rita and Stephanie. At the General Assembly the evening of December 10th after the 46 got out, some of the 1000 or so students that came to show their support at the Boston Commons tried to block the 46 from speaking, I guess this was because they felt guilty for not showing up the next day to defend the camp, as when they initially did, it stopped the police raid. John Ford was still able to speak known as the "leader" on camp, for his work with safety. Anna Aizman on facilitation from the GA unlike me did not try to silence him. He started by attacking the audience, that they should be ashamed of themselves, not just for not showing up to defend camp but for trying to silence those who went to jail for them. But the speech I wrote that night took a different approach. I thought before I spoke, of Dewey Square, where we lived, now shut off, of the philosopher John Dewey it was named after, who formed the Dewey Commission in defense of Leon Trotsky, exiled and defamed, Trotsky, a revolutionary, was vindicated as a result. Was this speech to be my vindication after a life of being silenced?

Thanks to David Lumoso's intervention, Anna backed off and let me speak at the GA, this was the first time I realized she was hostile to me. I told the audience that we must continue the fight to a American

13

Spring, that I am homeless, with nothing to lose, that I was told if I went to speak to them on the Gazebo of the Boston Commons that night that I would be arrested and kept in jail till we went to court, but so be it, the revolution was born in Boston and it will be reborn in Boston, to my surprise there was a standing ovation. I remembered the vision I had that summer in Boston that I would speak to a crowd at the Gazebo. I remembered talking to my sister that a revolution was coming. My dreams seemed to be coming true. David came and apologized to me for not speaking to me earlier when I got out of jail to a applauding crowd with coffee and donuts waiting for us, that I had balls, sadly like with Branden, I had a fallout with David, and he even seemed on my side when the allegations came out, but I guess it was too much drama for him.

Then John Ford spoke again, this time using my words, changing his approach, talking about locking arms with his brothers and sisters, Anna looking at me while he said it in mic check. For those of you who don't know that term, it was invented in NYC, AKA Peoples Mic, because the cops prohibited people from using a speaker phone you say a few words and the crowd repeats, like "My name is Al" and the crowd says "My name is Al" and so on and so forth. It works well for certain things, but of course we don't want to use it too much, especially to strangers, who may think we are a cult. John had already discredited himself a couple times, I found out when we were in DC he was working to dismantle camp through the GA, and he was the only one of the 20 some people locking arms to get up, but to be fair, he came back in the end and sat next to me in the patty wagon. I never had any issues with John ran into him at a few protests, but recently I found he is off my friends list on Facebook, another guy who could not handle the drama. Perhaps as a result of this book more people will want to reconcile, as events have vindicated me somewhat already. I am outspoken, but so are most activists, it should not be a sin to be so outspoken you are not popular or make some enemies, be judged by your actions, the content of your character, not your race, sex or outspokenness. There was only 2 of the 46 that spoke that night in Boston, my credibility as we went to court was high, I brought people to tears, was one of the most respected activists at that point, for them to go after my reputation the lies against me would have to be most grotesque. But that is what they do through history. The "they" I will get into later. I remember now before the cop stomped on me to break my arms from my comrades how I gave one of the last mic checks, I said I wanted to give a shout-out to Occupy Vermont, that I am here for my country, for the future of my country, and for all our children. My voice was weak from all the chants in the rain in DC but it still rang through and finally I could be heard.

Chapter 6 New Years In New York With Occupy

My first time at Freedom Plaza AKA Zuccotti Park (not to be confused with Liberty Plaza at Occupy DC) where the movement was born was actually after the camp already fell, it was the day before New Years Eve. The first place I heard about was the Atrium which is a place right on Wall Street where occupiers hanged out, it was basically a lobby with some Palm trees where occupiers would eat, but whenever anyone slept not sitting up security would wake them up, which I found stupid, I was actually able to cover myself up and sleep on my side a bit there for a nap, sleeping in a church one night, and a "safe house" in Brooklyn the next. Safe house is not to be confused with a squat, which is a foreclosed home occupiers can sleep in, which I hear were also in Brooklyn along with global revolution studios where live-feed video people were raided. The cool thing about those spots is you wake up in the morning and can talk of politics over coffee, I live to exchange views and fine commonalities, not just on politics, but history, passionate issues in general.

14

This was at the height of the occupier housing crisis, just a few weeks after they were raided, they were still coordinating where to send homeless occupiers, I heard some went to "occupy farms" in Vermont. I would later be back in NYC at Union Square where occupied moved in late March, urging the homeless to join our "army" in the New Haven camp during the war against the homeless there by other occupiers, known as the "Occupy New Haven Civil War", which all started with a homeless occupier I defended, a woman who was sexually assaulted on camp by a sex offender, but that is a later story. New Years' Eve a woman named Heather shows up with a little tent she snuck into the park, where her children are inside. I join a small group of people locking arms around the tent. In my mic check I said I give a shout-out to Occupy Boston, and that I am ready to be arrested again. I texted Stephanie and Jason in Boston who urged me not to get arrested.

The small group consisted of a woman named Gismos, she was about 19 but very mature, in her eccentric way, she had a brief relationship with me, almost bringing her back to Boston, sometimes I think things would have been different if I did, she was part Puerto Rican part Trinidadian, large, outgoing, who had a pet rat she brought everywhere. She said she had an arrest warrant for defending her sister, she escaped from jail and was looking for her sister who also escaped, I thought she was incredibly brave, I later found out she was back in prison, no word on her sister. Also an illegal immigrant was locking arms with us. Finally a deal was made for no one was allowed in or out of the park. Freedom of movement was brought back in exchange for the tent, the mother agreed, and tensions calmed down, for the moment. I hugged her and said I was willing to give my life for her children like I was for my niece, the daughter of my late sister. I then sat down and cried right there in the park. This scene all happened right after a General Assembly in that same park.

During the ordeal I saw in the distance two people from Boston, James, and his girlfriend Anna, my problems with them later basically all of Occupy Boston knew about, but at that point we were friends.

I told them I was going to be arrested again, they looked shock to see me, James, who calls himself a veteran (he admitted to me he did not make it past basic training) had a flag, and he bravely charged the police to get into the park, as they claimed his flag was a threat because of the medal pole. This restarted the tensions with the police. During the whole ordeal he somehow didn't get arrested, but I didn't either, we were lucky. We marched to the golden bull statue near Wall Street which had a police barricade around it and police guarding it. It made me think of the biblical figure of the golden calf in the Sinai, the devilish worship of money, or later, of the golden elephant we made to protest the Republican National Convention in Tampa. When we were marching back to the park I yelled to James that is Wall Street! Part of it had been barricaded off since occupy started. Police did not outnumber us, many were guarding Times Square for New Years.

So we took advantage and James with his flag ended up leading the charge, even some NY occupiers asked us not to, as well as the cops, but the Boston radicals moved forward (at least most of us, James was from Vermont) we went up to the steps of a building on Wall Street celebrating, and marched down to the Fed building, running into more comrades from Boston on the way, as the rest of the occupiers followed behind us, we were on the front-lines where it all started! Among those we ran into was Nunes of Occupy Boston, Nunes is a 17 year old man from Brazil, I say man as he proved himself to be one even with such a young age, while we did tug of war with the cops on the barricades, right beside me as a covered my face, he took a direct hit of peppery spray back at the park, that's Mayor Bloomberg's hospitality, from his "private army" as he called the NYPD at MIT. Luckily medics

15

attended to it soon after using water to clear his eyes, but were still red. We were restarting the movement for the New Year! We sang on the steps of the Fed building catching our breath, and headed back to Freedom Plaza. Then the cops grabbed a guy off his bicycle, and we attempted a de-arrest, to impede the cops from throwing him in the patty wagon, I yelled to James what was going on, and we charged, him still with the flag in his arms. I had my lucky backpack on, a cop grabbed me from behind and a jolt of adrenaline hit me making me twist to the side throwing the cop away from me on to someone else. I don't know how many got thrown in the patty wagon but James and I were in one piece.

Finally we took down most of the barricades around the Plaza, especially at the front, and started building "mount liberty" which I heard had been done before. We danced on that mountain of barricades, I can be seen with a blue jacket and backpack in many videos of the seen, singing, we had the taste of freedom, if only temporary. A man handed me a bottle of vodka to make my resolution revolution for the New Year, this man I later ran into in New Haven, Don Montano, a homeless occupier, he was part Italian part Portuguese, a short man with glasses in his late 30s, his grandfather started the mob in New Haven.

Don was accompanied by a man who was later to become my ally, Ty Hailey, both were plaintiffs with me on the injunction to keep the occupation at the Green in New Haven under respected attorney Norm Pattis, prior to that Irving Pinsky was representing us, he told me he saw the civil war on camp as a Stalin-Trotsky feud, and I saw some similarities. Especially in regards to Ben Aubin's security group and its cult of personality, but I will tell that later. It's funny since in Vermont I had a friend named Hailey (the one detained during the raid) and another named Tyler, similar to Ty Hailey' name. I also met a Dominican veteran, a marine, who I would see get arrested in my next trip to NY, he told me that when he was arrested New Years he was in a short time since he is a soldier. Funny since Jason released with me came out around the same time as the rest of us but that's Boston.

I eventually fell asleep on mount liberty, around 1am I woke up to police around me, my instincts said walk out, don't run, if you run they get you, even with chaos around you. I was right and I saw James and Anna from a distance arguing with the cops. I then called Allegra, of Occupy Wall Street, she deals with housing, she helped me get to the church where I ran into Richard, who I had not seen since he came to Occupy Boston from Vermont to work on safety. I caught up with Allegra and others we took the train to the prisoner solidarity rally to go to the precinct where the comrades were just sent. Allegra apparently got word from Boston about the allegations against me not realizing who I was and when I reminded her she claimed to be afraid of me. It's sad she was so fearless when the cops took her down and I tried to help her, but against a fellow comrade a few lies can intimidate someone. The comrade from Brooklyn who took me in that night was with the people defaming me in Tampa recently but I got him to back off, it's amazing how people can turn against you, with no evidence, just out of fear.

Cindy of Occupy Miami I helped that night as well, and the rumors against me also had her not be my friend. But this is what happened. As we marched to where Cindy's boyfriend was being held, as he was right by me, who goes by Kobra (it is interesting to note at a protest in Tampa I ran into another Kobra, who said that the Miami Kobra was pissed he had the same nom-de-guerre, I had known Cindy and Kobra from Boston, NY and later ran into them in DC), we were "kettled" or what is more

16

commonly known as cornered by the cops. Ashley Carter, who I heard recently left occupy, was arrested in Boston, NY and DC, she was that night at a safe house in Brooklyn and through her Cindy and I were able to get out.

The first round of cornering there was about 75 of us, they surrounded us with scooters, and let us out one by one, as helicopters had traced our movement. Then some of the group left, and there was about 50 of us left, just before the second cornering I asked Allegra if she wanted a drink, she was not feeling well, she said yes, I ran into a store to get her juice, and as soon as the cops started circling I ran through the scooters to get her the juice. Then the cops told us to disperse, my instincts said stay put. They started grabbing people, throwing them on the ground, there was blood, I saw Allegra went down, I went to the corner, Cindy's friend, a black man, was told by a female cop he could not smoke, she flicked the cigarette out of his mouth, and threw him to the ground of the cement floor, Cindy told me she could not get arrested, I told her to stay with me.

Finally there was about 10 of us left, and the cops told us to raise our hands if we wanted out. Then they continued to grab people. We walked up to the cops and said we were just coming through as if not occupiers, I normally would not do that but I did it for Cindy, I figured she did not need the trouble, but they told us to stay, in the end, there was only about three of us who got out, Cindy and I included. Cindy, me and another woman kept marching but the cops took pity on us that is the type of determination to start revolutions. Cindy needed to use the bathroom but the snobs of NY said she had to buy something, she eventually found a bathroom. We sat down my cell was dead with Ashley's number, suddenly she remembered Kobra's cell was in her bag, with Ashley's number, it was like 3am, luckily Ashley answered, and she told us how to get to Brooklyn, as Cindy dossed off on the train I awoke her to our stop. I slept in the basement that night, on a sleeping bag like a good occupier. The next day Cindy and I got a hold of Kobra and their friend bailed out by the NLG, the lawyers union, and a few comrades from Boston where there too, I had seen Cindy at the church a couple days back and thought she was from Boston not Miami. Then it was off to DC.

Chapter 7 In DC For Ashley

Ashley liked to hitchhike she was a hippie, much like my mother was, but she also was like a gypsy, liked to move around a lot. She came from California. Like my father, her father sent her money from abroad, she was half American and half Vietnamese, the Vietnamese on her mother's side, she looked Latina, she was slender, in her early 20s, with an innocent look on her, but you could tell she liked to have a good time. But I would have none of it. I insisted Greg Murphy from the Occupy Boston finance committee; get us Megabus passes from New York to DC so we could travel together, had she not deserved it? The good thing about Megabus was not just the price but that all we had to do was give a code to get on it, it was direct, comfortable with Wi-Fi, a lot of us homeless people did not have IDs. Ashley had been arrested three times for the movement. Who knew if some crazy old man would pick her up hitchhiking and do something to her.

17

So we arrived back in DC, I had not been there since the National GA the month before. There was an event in DC later that month, Occupy Congress, which Stephanie and a group sponsored by the Boston GA went to after she left Occupy Manchester, NH, but I was not able to go to it because of the allegations in Boston. I got to see the tensions between McPherson and Liberty Plaza, the two rivaling camps, and how they planned to cover it up during Occupy Congress, much like the tensions of the West Tampa Camp and Romneyville Camp here in Tampa.

I got to meet Thi while I was in DC, she went to court with Ashley, she got arrested at the Supreme Court one day, I later saw a picture of this arrest, seeing how she was carried out, and was quite impressed. She stayed in the same tent as me but we did not spend the night together, as I went to see my friend Celeste in Virginia, later in May around her birthday I was able to help her get to see Noam Chomsky in Boston, what a humble man. Thi was also part Vietnamese like Ashley, I could tell she liked me as we walked together at a museum, but she was mad that I did not spend the night in the tent I was designated to, or respond to her texts, as my cell got lost.

I was set up in the medic tent at Liberty Plaza but I wanted to go back to McPherson like I did the month before, which was not far away, that was the anti-war camp and known as the more radical of the two. I also got to meet one of my heroes, Medea Benjamin, founder of the feminist group Codepink, now here were real feminists, willing to go as far as the Middle East to fight with what they believe in, against the injustice of Zionism in Gaza, etc. Medea later came on my online radio show and I ran into her a couple times in Tampa during the protests.

Medea had gone to Gaza with Ridgely Fuller, who was arrested with me, her mug-shot was just above mine on the front page of the Boston Herald along with other comrades, like Rita, James, Stephanie, Branden, etc, which had one article in favor of us, another against, the one in favor called us patriots, had a quote from me, that I got arrested since I was fed up with the injustice, that reporter had called me when I was with Richard at my Nana's house, right after doing a second interview with Univision which never aired. When your camp shuts down the press usually does not want to talk to you, only when it's around. I remember when I was being arrested I saw Ashley with the other women in the patty wagon and I called out her name with a big smile on my face as she saw me, she says she does not remember, some things get blocked out. She was another California heartbreaker like Brianna, who used to come to our camp to use the hoola hoops, I had stayed with her the first night I got out of jail.

Ashley started a relationship with a guy at camp in DC, but it was not serious, she refused to call him her boyfriend, but he liked to think he was. Ashley and I finally ran into Kobra, Cindy, and their friend, they were passing through and were on their way back to Miami (with a stop at Occupy Orlando). She would have went back with them but she had to stay in DC to do community service as part of the deal she took. I later found out Cindy, who so determined to see her boyfriend out of jail went on a march with me and almost got arrested, broke up with her boyfriend in Miami, I heard drugs were involved, drugs can cause so much destruction to a relationship and a movement.

Even at regionals in the Ocala National Forest of Rainbow Gathering, where 99% of the people use drugs, besides a few drinks, I did not use any substance. Mike Madison, a acquaintance from Tampa, accompanied me with a small group from occupy to Rainbow, I was hanging out with a black woman one night, as we were there for three nights, and suddenly Kitty, a woman from Tampa, recognized me, grabbed the person I was with and claimed I assaulted her in some way. I found the woman the next day and brought her back Mike Madison asked if I was disrespectful at all and she said no, but Kitty

18

continued her defamation against me under the influence of many people and having suffered apparently from a trauma of her own. I had in fact just missed Ashley at Rainbow and Tampa, I had to go back to Boston for court, then would be in New Haven, would have been nice to see her. After DC I saw Ashley briefly in Boston that would be the last time I saw her, we kept in touch online or by cell from time to time but it was hard since my number changed every few months. So it was back to Boston with a brief stop in NY, where Heather at the church gave me a big hug and called me Boston Al, and Gismos was there, and we snuggled together at the church. From the Atrium the next day she told me she could not go back with me and we said our goodbyes.

Chapter 8

The Deaths of "Chief" & Brian Arredando

Upon the return to Boston the movement was in chaos over the ongoing Level 3 Sex Offenders proposal which I will delve into in the next chapter. What's worse, the death of a homeless occupier, Chief, was announced, he was on the cold streets of Boston after camp was shutdown, many of us felt guilty, I had warned people without solidarity there would be deaths after camp was shutdown, some occupiers were in the hospital with him when he gave his last breathe. Branden started crying and I gave him a big hug. At that GA James was there and gave me a big hug, I had not seen him since NY. I had joined the spiritual working group and a woman and me had a moment of silence to calm everyone down when we announced our group. I could not stand the drama at that meeting, since as I tended to do, I left early, but with the intention of returning. I went back to Jamaica Plain to my room my Dad had made sure I got, with a crazy Greek landlady; I changed clothes, and got a haircut, by the time I returned a conclusion on the Level 3 Sex Offenders proposal had been made.

Women were outside upset, and it was what I had feared. The proposal did not go through. I found out an outsider, a man who had only attended two General Assemblies, and who hid the fact he was part of a rape advocate group who "rehabilitated" rapists, was able to block the proposal, I planned to reform the block but allegations against me prevented me from bringing this proposal. In fact it would have been my first, my former proposal, to take my trip in the name of Occupy Boston, I forfeited so the controversial proposal on banning people would be considered. I felt levels 3s were a big threat, that we could not permit them from coming to our gatherings. My plan was this, if in Boston you wanted a train pass, a bus pass, anything from the finance committee, you had to be signed off by two working groups. I thought why not, to have the power of the block, you have to be signed off the same way? To be a member of a working or affinity group? Some occupies had gotten rid of the block altogether, as a consensus based group, if 10% of the people found your block to be of principle, you were able to block a proposal when it came time for the vote. That was a lot of power to give someone. Percentages differed from different occupies. Anyway I will get into more of that later. Just days after Chief died we got word at another GA that Brian Arredando, son of Carlos Arredando, had killed himself. I immediately tried to find out who they were, and I found out they were friends with Jason and lived in Jamaica Plain where I did, the wake was in fact down the street from where I lived but I could not go to it, too emotional, nor the funeral, I was able to put myself together and attend a vigil, I believe it was the next night after we found out about his death and I was able to talk to Carlos about the death of my sister, and my niece, how she kept me living, how we were all his family. But no words can alleviate the pain, all his sons were dead, with no grandchildren, and my only sibling was dead.

19

Brian grew depressed after the death of his brother Alex in Iraq, and he locked himself in a room and killed himself, as I almost did in Georgia, before my sadness turned to anger when my mother kicked me out, with a will to live that would maintain me. I saw Stephanie at the vigil, hugged her, and told her I liked her poem on why we got arrested, that we loved too much, she had tears in her eyes, I loved her so much in that moment, I remembered when I told her about my sister in the gert where we rested, I felt so close to her, but things got complicated in the end.

An example of how Stephanie stood up for people, there was a Jewish lady who took in Bobbi, a homeless occupier lady, and Bobbi complained she was exploited and that she made her use her food stamps and work in exchange for staying with her. Stephanie found out about this from Bobbi as Bobbi was crying, this lady was going to take me in before I rented a room, but she did not as she blamed the incident on me, knowing I was friends with Stephanie. What ended up happening was at a Chinese restaurant there was a occupy meeting and the manager ordered Branden and other homeless comrades out, Stephanie and I were mad about it, and Stephanie ran in and yelled a mic check against the lady while I was outside.

The lady cursed at Stephanie and ran out, saying it was my fault. Stephanie felt guilty and helped me find shelter that night. To be fair this lady told me she was a Zionist, so there had been some tensions building up with the movement, she was also a Democrat and was accused of being a co-opter, I forget her name but the first time I spoke to Occupy Boston at a GA was through the working group I was trying to form with her, I told Boston how I came from Vermont and strived to learn from them to build a new society. Allison was facilitating that night, she later got arrested with us, in-spite of threats from Phil on camp. Later the three of us (Stephanie, the Jewish lady and I) made up when we returned to Dewey Square when it was reopened after it was shut down and cleaned up, having a spiritual event there. Bobbi went on to lead the homeless working group which I attended a couple times. I later found out Tyler in Vermont had known Carlos Arredando. But he was not able to make it to Boston then.

Later the old Greek lady brought a Greek kid to take over my room, she did not want me there anymore, as I was to move to Providence, I was friendly with him anyway, I told him getting arrested for Occupy Boston against all odds was like the 300 Spartans against the Persian invaders, he liked that analogy.

Chapter 9

Level 3 Sex Offenders Proposal

Before I delve into the allegations made against me on January 10th, soon after my return from trips back when occupy paid for the Megabus fares, to NYC for the Occupy New Years event, and to Occupy DC in solidarity with Ashley Carter who was going to court for doing CD (civil disobedience), and just a couple days after my late sister's birthday, it must be understood the implications of the bringing of the banning of level 3 sex offenders from our gathering and how it was blocked from an

20

outsider, causing division and paranoia up to when false accusations were made against me without my presence at a General Assembly. I was in favor of the proposal. Even making myself a male ally of the Womens Caucus of Occupy Boston in the process, as I had walked out with them upon finding out the result of the GA when I returned.

Demonetization was brought which I was against, the others were called the "pro rape group" I later found out Brian Kwoba had made an alternative proposal, that was softer, to be fair he was out of the country for the holidays and was unaware of a lot that was going in, this did not stop my friendship with him. Since the attempt to kick a known belligerent, Phil, out of camp in Boston through GA process, as I voted to kick him out but a block by a tight vote had him stay, we needed some type of proposal, especially to protect children, as there had been a level 3 sex offender on our camp who attempted to go to our meetings after it was shut down, I worked on safety and had no knowledge of this.

It was actually David who first found out when he came with the jail support group when we got out, and the cops gave him a paper that had a list of sex offenders who stayed on our camp, David later announced this at GA, and the Womens Caucus planned this proposal, I think the cops had this all

planned to divide us. I remember when Jason drove me to South Station when I was going to NY, as I could not get on the train in time to catch the bus, I told him what was going on in GA, as he had not been attending, and while I was gone he decided to show up and speak in favor of the proposal, he like me, thought it was a no brainer, and had been dragged on too long, causing division, that there should be a vote, and that should be the end of it. I was warned that this proposal could be used against innocents, even people who were not sex offenders, I refused to believe that,
ironically a similar measure was used against me when I had done so much to defend the women who brought this proposal forward, never in my worst nightmares could I have imagined the outcome.

Chapter 10 Allegations

For many this is the first time you hear my side of the story, you have heard many conflicting reports, you may skip to this chapter just to read this part, I suggest you don't, there is a chronology here that is very important that shows how events led up to this. So on the night of January the 9th, having spent the previous night alone in my room depressed since it was to be my sister's 26th birthday, I decided to go out the next night with whatever group of occupiers I could find, I thought, why not with James & Anna? Their group, the "gypsy squad" would let me go, since I proved I was a worry comrade in NY, Boston & DC. So we went to the "occusafehouse" in Mattapan, where Eli Holmes and the medics stayed. However, there was a couple things that raised my suspicion of them I blocked out of my mind. Number 1 James was a huge guy, and he seemed the jealous type, as many men from Vermont are. 2 in NY during a break of the protests I mentioned in a mic check I was arrested for the movement, and he gave a twinkle fingers down.

For those of you who don't know what that is, when you agree you twinkle your fingers at any time in occupy up, disagree, down. I made a joke once that an occupier guy goes on a date to the movies with a non-occupier girl, he sees a scene he likes, does the twinkle fingers, and the girl says, who are you waving at?! Anyway James doing that was the first sign he was jealous of me and a sign it would be a mistake to hang out with them. He was ungrateful, he would say thanks to a worker at a t stop (train

stop) for letting him in for free for being a occupier but I don't remember him ever thanking me for using my food stamps to give him and his friends food, nor thinking Stephanie when she bought them food. Ironically, James and Anna were defenders of Phil, they said he had enemies on camp since he was outspoken, it was rumored that Phil was working for the cops to disrupt camp, later I was to make enemies with them, in part for being outspoken with a few drinks in me. I said to James all Vermonters are hillbillies except for those from Burlington, I was saying it as a joke but he took it the wrong way.

Anyway, Anna had her credit card (ironically a Bank of America card, "anarchists" like to break the windows of those places, but don't divest and join a credit union like many comrades did including myself) and needed someone to walk to the liquor store with her who had a ID, I volunteered, no one else wanted to go with us. We bought a bottle of whiskey and got lost on the way back, Anna called James to help give us directions, we walked through a park and finally found our way back, we were gone about an hour, while we talked I told Anna about my sister, and she seemed very sympathetic.

Someone suggested the next day she made up a story against me from the party to convince her jealous boyfriend there was nothing going on between us. Anna was very young, the witch-hunt she started against me must have been conducted by the descendants of the Salem Witch Trials themselves, which those who know the story were started by young girls who made gossip against innocent God-fearing people.

So we got back and opened the bottle of whiskey. I got a cup of ice, Anna had not eaten much and I did not want her to get drunk, I shared the cup with her. We later all passed out on the floor. I gave Anna a hug before I went to sleep, I remember everything, I did not touch or say anything inappropriate to her. For all her convincing to James there was nothing between us I found out they broke up months later, Anna kicked James out and he was homeless again, around that time James and I made up, I took pity on him.

The GA of January 10th, the next evening, was the worst ever for Occupy Boston in my opinion, worse than when the proposal was blocked, not just for what was said against me when I left early and was not able to defend myself. Zoe, whom I am cool with now, a transgender or whatever she likes to be called, is the one who made the announcement against me. Allison, and other members of the Womens Caucus, walked out when Angela, the facilitator, had tried to silence one of their members. Before that, I spoke up saying I am for unity but we must differentiate between occupier and occupy supporter, that I did not know who this outsider was who blocked the proposal at the last GA, but that something should be done about it. When I saw Allison and the others leave, I followed them, I asked if Allison was coming back in she said no. Then I saw James and his friends, outside, he looked very upset. I asked him, bro, what's wrong? He said I know what I did.

I thought to myself, I might have said something stupid at the party that got him upset and he wanted to confront me about it at GA. Not wanting to confront a fellow occupier and fed up with the drama, I left the church where the meeting was held from the other side of the building, there was a daycare there and we were not supposed to exit that way, but the guy who guarded the door knew I was a respected activist, and I explained to him it looked like a fight was going to happen on the other side, so he let me through. God knows what James would have done to me if I stayed, or maybe I would have been able to defend myself better, who knows, the what-ifs drive you mad. After I left Zoe came in and this is pretty much what she said to the shock of all: "We have evidence last night Al Suarez ruffied a occupier at a party, she has decided to remain anonymous, we are looking for him!". For those of you

22

who don't know a ruffy is a drug used to rape women. Such an accusation was against everything I am. I was not informed of it till the next day, all I knew was that allegations were made against me, I went to the E 5 building (Ecuentro Cinco) in Chinatown, where occupiers frequent to find out what they were, when I was told. I was in shock.

At first I thought they really did a test, that they really had evidence and really thought it was me since I was the "outsider" of the group. Later I found out there was no evidence and this got me angry, I confronted James about this outside a GA once and barely got away before he came to beat me, I walked away though, with pride, saying: "Where is the evidence?!" I went to police headquarters but there was no report. I will now show you what an advocate of mine read for me later at a GA, then I will explain from what I alluded to earlier as "they" or in the statement as "outside forces", and the difference between paranoia and vigilance, as well as the evidence that backs up the assertion of infiltrators in our movement like in other movements who came in to disrupt our movement.

"I generally believe those who talk a lot do little so to not use up the GA's time I will make this as brief as possible.

First I want to state that I hope Sage is given the right to read this. Sage barely knows me, is unbiased, but he is my brother in spirit as all those who are part of Occupy Boston. Mind you I have not tried to enter today, I was informed before hand I would be investigated, but up to the moment of writing this safety has still refused to question me, perhaps because they like the cops, the pharmacy, and the hospital, know this is bogus.

Yesterday I talked to Zoe in E-5, this was before I read the transcript and realized it was this same person who did the mic check against me in the last GA in my absence. Zoe told me that the people who accused me provided no evidence to her. After she calmed down, heard me out, she said if she sees no evidence she will back off. She should be more angry than me, they used her trauma, and hid behind her outside while she came in and did the mic check, she was exploited for the purpose to try to ruin my reputation in the movement, which has been exemplary up till now. The people who have accused me have no proof that I put a ruffy in a drink and gave it to a woman at a party, in-spite of the fact the woman nor her friends accused me of touching or saying a single bad word to her-that night, in fact I was nice to her and everyone. I do not believe the woman in question who decided to remain anonymous is intentionally trying to ruin my reputation, outside forces, I won't say whom, have stirred people-up against me somehow, we were friendly up till recently. When I talked to one of my accusers outside the last GA as I saw he was upset, I wanted to find out what was going on, but he refused to tell me, nobody did till two days ago where I immediately went to E 5 to find out what was going on where I ended up threatened, I was told I would be beaten till I told the truth, I wonder, if the government tortures us into telling the truth, will this person than realize I am his brother?

I talked to the police and found out there was no evidence, eventually finding out there was no police report, the hospital and the pharmacy confirmed no such test for ruffys existed, they started out with lies which right there takes away their credibility. While I was at E 5 I was able to go online briefly, I saw that Anna Aizman from safety, had written on the 46 Facebook group I started, 46 for the amount of people arrested at Dewey's last stand, , myself and other brave souls included.

23

This is where I first heard that I would not be allowed back into GAs or working group meetings till safety investigated me, in the Orwellian tone I was told I had to do this voluntarily, but we all know what that means. From that moment in countless comments and requests of people I begged someone from safety to come to E 5 to question me. This was never done and I was eventually asked to leave E 5 which I did with no resistance.

I don't know why Miss Aizman has a personal vendetta against me, she wanted to silence me when I tried to speak at GA the day I got released from prison with the 45 others, but David made sure I could speak to the crowd. I joined safety because of people like Phil who was given more rights than me and was able to plead his case from the beginning. I joined safety to defend people like Miss Aizman who was called a Nazi by Phil, which I found particularly hurtful since she is a Jew. My only sibling, my younger sister, died shortly before this movement started, she told me in a dream to move forward in this movement for my niece, a 3 year old whose safety I am concerned about all the time.

It saddens me to say that some of the people I defended, as I was in favor of the proposal against the level 3s, these women I cried with, hugged, and defended till the end, these same women who gave me the honorary title of male ally, women like Allison who I came to express my support when Phil threatened her, I said she was a brave woman, she would return to GA, she did, and was one of the 46, her husband Greg must be so proud of her. I refused to believe Allison took part in what other individuals did recently, they sent my photo out to other occupies so I cannot take part anymore. I went all the way to DC to be the only member of Occupy Boston to show solidarity in court with Ashley, who was arrested at Dewey, NY and DC, when she is arraigned in New York it seems I won't be able to be there for I have no money for a hotel and the Church won't take me from these photos. This is irreparable damage even if I take these people to court and a statement is sent out saying I am innocent the damage is done.

Zuccotti where on New Years' I defended a woman's children in a small tent, I told her I would give my life for her children like I would for my niece, I broke down and had no one at Zuchotti to hold me, but I made friends there. We built a mountain of liberty with the barricades no one can take that moment from me or deny I was there. They called me Boston Alex when they thought of Boston they thought of me with affection, I represented you, I was cornered, persecuted, that night, by the NYPD, as they hauled my comrades away like cattle, including women, who I came to defend. Only to come home to Boston and be singled out by the comrades I left to represent with all my love and respect. This movement gave me hope which I must not lose. Is this a inquisition or a GA?

The government uses the words homeland security to justify silencing people, the only difference is it's called safety now among us as I cannot even read my own statement. When we had a camp at times I slept in Stephanie's tent, taking refuge there never once was I disrespectful towards her, even when I had a few drinks in me. When I worked safety I never drank was respectful to everyone. I am the type of man who will take his shirt off for you, who won't be afraid to jump in front of a car for you. Like the other 45, those who sat in front of a bulldozer, in front of snipers in the Fed building, those 20 locking arms against over 200 specially trained cops ready to beat us. The only one to get up from the 20 was John Ford, I gave a mic check after his, convincing everyone to stay, saying we were doing this for our children. When Gunner after I got out of jail, said at a meeting he wanted to leave the movement, I said if anyone did they would let the 46's sacrifice go in vain. No one left that day. I was among the few to plead not guilty, we were back on Dewey as soon as it opened up having a spiritual gathering, some of those same people were in New York with me New Years.

24

The spirit of my sister lives in all the women who fight for their rights. Che said if you cringe with indignation at any injustice, than you are a comrade of mine, all of you who sense this injustice done to me, if you do nothing now, know you could be next, I have a clean record, let my actions speak for themself. Even in Plato's Apology we see Socrotes was able to defend himself, probably most in the room knew he was innocent, but he was given a choice, death or exile, he chose death, I have been in self-exile it's not a good thing at times. Is this a Greek tragedy or a comedy? Right after speaking against the block of the proposal, I leave the controversy, not knowing why my accusers are mad at me, and then I am accused of this. We need to end the paranoia, we need to be vigilant yes, but we must let the forces of love prevail. One of my accusers even in the heat of the moment I said he had a right to be angry. I may have had a slip of the tongue if it was my girlfriend too we are human we have emotions not just logic.

But we need to stop infighting for this is a favor to the system we are trying to fight. I have a right to defend myself, as even Socrotes did. Nor Miss Aizman nor anyone should be able to take away that right. If the GA wants me to leave I will respect that decision. But remember these words. Most of all remember all I did for the movement."

Sage did a good job reading the statement that fateful day in January, as I watched him read the end of it on live-feed, he even had some of my mannerisms, we talked for several hours before he went to read it, I told him my life was in his hands. There was no interruption of the statement I heard about, in fact people applauded, one of those who applauded was "Bil" Lewis, who I would later host in Tampa for the RNC protests, I also hosted Sparro, who I would meet later in NY and bring with me to New Haven, a brave woman with many talents. I will now describe in further detail what I meant by outside forces and "them", and what they have done to the movement.

Outside sources in particular are what have always been known in movements as agent provocateurs, those paid by an agency or coerced by an agency or group, into infiltrating a movement and sabotaging it by means of rumor, divisive disruption, and other things, letting people get trapped into emotion rather than logic. They do more than observe. Chiefs of Police have admitted to sending undercover cops, the FBI have set up occupiers (see Cleveland and Chicago cases), and homeland security agents will be testifying against Occupy Boston, no doubt these agents in our midst all use similar tactics and in hindsight can or will be recognized. What is to be done to get rid of this poison in the movement? Many blame the problems of occupy on random acts of violence by "black bloc anarchists" who are mostly upper middle class white kids with an axe to grind.

Nevertheless, I think they are just convenient scapegoats, when they came to protest the RNC in Tampa they caused little problems. Are some of them agents? It's possible. Others believe what they are doing is helping things. Non-violence is the way, and I feel most still in the movement are for non-violence. The best way to wipe out this filth is with leadership, direction, discipline and organization, some say they will leave the movement if this comes about, if we build a political party, so be it, this is necessary for the survival of the movement, a program of social justice must come about, a united front must be formed.

25

In the end we lacked conviction, we lacked unity, that is why Anna Aizman could so easily sabotage mediation and get people to make up stories against me of harassment and contact Occupy Vermont & Providence, and sabotage my activism in the US for months to come. That is why Eli Holmes could try to sabotage me in NY and at UMASS, when I came with OWS (Occupy Wall Street) and Providence people to that school, as described in the next chapter. Countless activists have received similar accusations against them and were treated like me or worse many of them were respected activists in their communities, and for precisely that reason they were targeted.

My last Occupy Boston event was on Martin Luther King Day, I helped host it with The People of Color Working Group, my advocate Brian Browne made sure I was there, I will always remember, Branden was there, Sage, Brian Kwoba, we called the two Brians Brian K and Brian B, we were all happy. There was 100s of occupiers there and no one made a fuss with my presence. But it was still too complicated at that point to attempt to go to a General Assembly or other events. I decided to go to

Providence where I knew "Ping Pong" would be waiting for me, it was just about an hour train ride away, I just needed for the snow to settle down, it was the end of January when I left.

Chapter 11 Providence

The first person I saw on camp was Ping Pong, she was happy to see me. She was unaware of my problems with Occupy Boston, which I was obliged to tell her about, luckily in the beginning she was supportive and was already respected by the people there. She was very paranoid and said they did it to me since I am a real activist, but later she backed off her support since many of her friends were my accusers, but nothing could be done about it by then. She had in fact spread rumors that my comrades Jose and Branden were cops, Jose was one of the 46 arrested in Boston as well, later he was with me in New Haven, but I will get into that later.

Safety on camp in Providence had a talk with me, and I was free to stay, I assured them I would try to go back to Boston to mediate, which I did several times to no avail, even to the point of threatening hunger strike from my tent in Providence, where mediation broke off. Of course Aizman as she threatened, finding out on Facebook I was planning to go to Providence, told safety there I had to go back to Boston, as she told me if I left Boston to there she would have to contact the camp, but I would not be intimidated, apparently she does not believe in freedom of movement.

I was at the camp in its last days and they were too preoccupied to deal with Boston drama, they knew I was arrested with Occupy Boston and told me they had sent comrades during the October raid, one of the safety guys, Jared Paul, treated me with respect, and I will never forget that. He did not want the camp to shut down and make a deal but the GA decided it there in the end, I respect them for they survived the winter, one of the last camps in New England, I ran into some Providence people later at the Rainbow Gathering in Florida.

I had made a friend who was a occupy supporter and luckily was able to stay with him on the very cold nights, and there was a café near by where I warmed up in the mornings from camp, sometimes I could not get through to him so I went to a shelter, it was not a nice shelter, I had in fact lost my Russian hat I wore when I was arrested in Boston. Although I did run into a former member of the camp in Boston and informed him of Chief's death. He knew he was sick but not that he died.

26

One of the demands Occupy Providence had with the city was that a day shelter for the homeless be given, when the city offered this in exchange for them closing their camp they took their own camp down, I could not be there for long that day, I hated seeing occupiers doing that to themselves. While I was in Providence I also initiated mediation with Urszula of the Womens Caucus, or whatever her name, the director of the National Lawyers Guild of Massachusetts, what a mistake, she was very bias and in the end recommended I not return to Occupy Boston, she said she thought I was trying to force myself on the movement, apparently she does not believe in innocent till proven guilty. I heard she was detained in the October raid on Boston but immediately told the cops she headed the NLG and was released, if she wanted to do civil disobedience she would not have told them her identity like that. It was a conflict of interest anyway since the NLG represented me it was out of desperation for Aizman sabotaged prior "mediation". I was starting to think she was a Mossad agent she told people she was Russian but she had an Israeli passport, I was a known anti-Zionist in many activist circles. I mentioned this in a group once and a lot of people said I was crazy, only time will tell. Transparency is the enemy of the provocateurs, look at Assange.

While I was at Occupy Providence we formed a counter rally at the Statehouse against "pro-life" people over the abortion issue, some of the more radical activists throw from the top of the Statehouse condoms down while the priest spoke, I found it comical. It got heated but not physical, some of the security in the building gave us a hard time. One of the guys who filmed us from Occupy Providence I was to run into later on the Day of Action (February 28th) I went to the day after going to Occupy New Haven in New London, CT where I was to be arrested a second time for the movement. To see the conviction of some of the activists at Providence was inspiring, not just because they survived the winter as New Haven had, but because they even had a member in a wheelchair, all sorts of people would turn out.

Shortly before Occupy Providence was shut down a group of OWS people came straight from NY to our camp. They were on their way to Boston. I was excited. I saw this as an opportunity to vindicate myself, they were unaware of my problems with Occupy Boston, and even with Eli's defamation at UMASS they knew she was nuts and such lies spread against many in the movement, when I ran into them in NY later they gave me hugs, Stephanie must have put up a defense for me. This same Eli who spread my photo with lies against me on Twitter to various occupies who I almost made a law suite against. I brought the OWS people and a couple comrades from Providence to UMASS to show solidarity as their little indoor occupy was under threat, I pitched up my tent, Eli made a fuss, and I was kicked out, along with my tent, going back in a car with a comrade from Providence.

The most absurd thing is that Eli for the first time claimed I harassed her, when I was one of the few guys on camp in Boston she did not accuse of such a thing, I guess that was because people did not buy her "Al is a ruffier" bullshit she mentioned at GA there. She said for PR that I should go. In other words because of her anti-Al propaganda I could not be seen with her or near her medic tent, she is not even a student of UMASS, Jason and Stephanie prevented me being forcibly removed and helped mediate me leaving but they did not at any time say I should stay even though both of them knew I was coming.

27

In the rush of leaving I accidentally left my lap top, which Eli stole left in her tent and bragged about going through. I went back with a woman named Big Red from Providence, a redheaded woman in her 20s, not to be confused with her younger counterpart Little Red, a Hispanic woman, and Stephanie my comrade from Boston, was there said she would look for for my lap top, not initially finding it, after going through some of Eli's things, who luckily was not there, Stephanie found my lap top, which had photos of my sister, it would have been too much to lose it. Soon after the camp in Providence would be gone and I would be on my way back to Florida.

Chapter 12 Tampa

My trip back to Tampa, as I had been there before when I stayed with a cousin in Brandon, actually started with me flying to Orlando. Occupy Orlando was not much of a group anymore, so the next day I took a train at the invitation of Debbie King, to Tampa, where I brought my tent from Providence to the West Tampa Camp. It was a tent given to me from Providence hospitality, which I named after my sister, "Tasha's Tent", I got there the last day of January, and the day after Occupy Tampa members Marisol and Seth were arrested at a protest, Marisol particularly built a friendship with me and I loved practicing my Spanish with her. She is a Puerto Rican woman in her 40s, a widow with an 18 daughter, uninterested in occupy. Seth is a young man, with blonde hair, short, and passionate. Last time I saw him was at the Rainbow Gathering. Occupy Tampa is where I also first met J Lo and she told me stories of her experience with Occupy New Haven, I was to meet J Lo at other occupies later. J Lo is in her late 20s I believe, a transgender, and a Latina. She was picked on, on camp, and I stood up for her, giving me many enemies but who did not attack me till much later on.

My "Tampa Address" I read on camp, urging comrades to come to the defense of Occupy Miami who were under threat, is a suiting way to start this chapter, which I will post after explaining the scene of the camp a bit, the address did not have the effect I wanted but it did leave a good impression. Who would have known the infamous Tommy Parisi was at the raid in Occupy Miami and he was later to become my ally then enemy. So many characters to describe, some are not worth mentioning, others disgust me to mention. So I did not meet Parisi till later on. This camp was in its 4th week, previously there was no camp, just a few protesters with sleeping bags in downtown Tampa at Curtis Hixon, who would have thought I found out later Bruce Wright had helped the occupiers get the place in West Tampa, which was owned ironically by a strip club mogul, Joe Redner, it was small for a camp, by the projects, a known dangerous area, in "Voice of Freedom Park". It did not do much help in the end though that I was an "ally" of Bruce.

I was also to meet Joel & Kitty, initially friendly with me after Rainbow Gathering they turned into a sort of James & Anna characters to me, no doubt some Boston people who were hostile to me who were at Rainbow Gathering and briefly in West Tampa, had got word to Joel & Kitty with the allegations, but I will get into that later. I had done a radio interview with Tristan Lear AKA Trissy, and J Lo, while on camp, Trissy turned out to be incredibly two faced, openly gay, I used to tease him a little bit, even though I was straight, and he liked that, even in the heat of the moment he never said I harassed him, but out of "solidarity" with Kitty he turned on me.

28

I also met Zoe Alif, she was working at the live-feed studios New Years in New York, I told her my experience there, my fallout with Zoe much later as she did defend me for a while, ruined my relationship with Debbie who told me about the camp, it seems I don't have luck with people named Zoe. Also Mike Madison, a Cuban-Italian photojournalist (Madison is what he changed his last name to) also became friends with me, and he was with me at Rainbow and has turned into an ally, he was the man filming the arrests of Marisol and Seth. He was one of many comrades to have his heart broken by the movement, he may like Obama but nobody is perfect. Another interesting character is Susie, who Parisi and I later jokingly called the queen of occupy, or in Spanish "la reina de los indignados". She bought the campers some food and in exchange put a poster of herself on the fridge, she was a self-promoter who never spent a night on camp, whenever there were tensions and the question of someone to be kicked out came up, she was always at the forefront of getting rid of them, people like J Lo, Susie was on a power trip and took full advantage of occupy. I came to Tampa with my intentions pure. Trying to see the best in everyone. Here is what I said when I arrived there.

Tampa Address

By Al Suarez on Tuesday, January 31, 2012 at 2:22pm ·

We stand here today in defiance of a system that has oppressed us far too long, they have persecuted us, especially in the north, shut down our camps, but as I said in Boston, they may take our tents, but they cannot take our dignity! We won't let them take it! Solidarity and unity is crucial in these times of division and paranoia which has reached our movement from a corrupt society we strive to change. I write this address for individual stack at a GA upon arrival in Tampa or during an emergency meeting to deal with the Miami camp crisis. I need not say the importance of defending that camp, it is beyond question we must send as many comrades as possible to defend her as she is under threat, which is the duty of all occupiers, to support each other, in particular in times of need like this. I came from the northernest most major city Boston in the US, and will go to the southern most major city, Miami, Tampa is close, Tamiami, we must unite, from Orlando and other parts of Florida, we must have a united front. We must leave today and protect the Miami camp, leaving behind some comrades to spread the word, that we need people there. I respect this camp has its own rules, but we must adhere to the universal rules of justice as well, I accept fair laws, not unfair ones, we must again, strive for change, for a social justice we all seek.

Indeed, solidarity forever! I write this address from the train on my way to you, the train of revolution is upon us in this new year, a new consciousness is upon us in this last day of January. Like Lincoln who wrote his brief address on the train, I too am brief, for I firmly believe, in most cases, those who speak a lot do little, we must be men and women of action, and act on our human conscious collectively in this community and other occupy communities across the nation and world towards a new era, a new way out of this mess. We must dream the dreams of our forefathers for a more free and equal world where liberty and justice can be for all, as they fought to take off the shackles of British imperialism. Miami needs tents, needs most of all, a presence, we must build barricades, take down some, but all these actions are out of a revolution of love, let us not forget that, that this new society is an ideal we strive for in this ongoing struggle for a better future of this country and for all our children, that is why I was one of the 46 December 10th last year to be arrested at the last stand at Dewey Square in Boston, that is what I said in my mic check before the police stomped on my comrades and me.

29

I went also to show solidarity to Vermont, Providence, DC and New York, now back in the south I am confident we can work together in the east coast towards the unity we desire deep down in-spite of all the drama and intimidation imposed by the new order of the government, we must be above that, and be non-violent, with discipline, everyone has their role, my role led me to plead not guilty, not taking a deal when our old camp was opened back up I went there with other brothers and sisters in spirit. The camp is no longer there but our legacy is, our efforts are not in vain, we are the majority, no longer will the elite of 1% control us, we shall prevail!!

After reading that many things happened that are too traumatic for me to get into, perhaps in a second edition, the conclusion will mention many of these things, the next chapter is also incomplete.

After going to court in Boston upon returning from Tampa, I decided to go to another occupy camp, the last major camp in New England, New Haven. I arrived on the bus, and took a free Yale shuttle right to camp, the day before the Day of Action, on February 28th. First arriving at "Yellingsford" on the Green in New Haven, it was called that since the homeless there liked to yell at night. A man who goes by Big Mike, who would later turn out to be a good ally, brought me to the main occupy camp across the Green, where I met Josh, he had me sign the "Good Neighbor Policy" which basically said there is no drug or alcohol use on camp, people have to respect each other, etc. He brought me to a tent in a large tent where he and other comrades stayed, called "Russia", there was about 4 or 5 tents in it, it was covered over with blue tarp that had graffiti on it and signs around it. And I was in a big tent called "Headquarters" I believe, much of this have been blocked from my mind from the trauma so you have to bear with me. It was a cold tent, the smaller tents are warmer, but I had many blankets and the people that owned the tent, had left over food in it I could eat, like almonds. I met Danielle that night, and she showed me around a bit, showed me stores in town where I could get food, etc. There was a food tent on camp, a supply tent, etc.

I also met Don, we found out later we had run into each other before in New York, he was the one passing around the bottle on New Years with Ty. Ty would come one night and dance and have a good time with us in New Haven, he was first suspicious I was a cop, as I asked to borrow his phone and he said no, later telling me why, but we grew to trust each other and formed a bond that lasts till this day. The next day I was informed an action was planned, we were to go to a town near New London, CT to protest a corrupt corporation. There was comrades from Hartford, Providence, and other parts of New England, one of them was Cassie, a young blonde woman from Hartford, I had seen her at a march in Boston, she was to be arrested with us that day near New London, it was the ironic march which started at the Boston Commons where people dressed as 1 percenters and chanted: this is what plutocracy looks like! Instead of this is what democracy looks like! That's where I had first seen her and she confirmed she was there. Funny that day near New London Josh had a big 1 percenter pin on him. Our

30

arrest this time was to be a bit of a publicity stunt, but for a good cause. The protest started like I said, near New London, at the offices in a small town in Groton, of Pfizer Corporation who uses drugs to test "subjects" whether animal or human, and with ALEC, buys off our politicians. But gather get more into that let me share this. The following is an article I wrote when what was going on was still fresh in my mind which was written just a few days after I arrived.

"The Counter Culture: What Does Occupy Represent? What Problems Does It Currently Face?
March 5, 2012 at 1:58pm

When the occupy movement is facing problems, we must ask ourselves, in fact remind ourselves, what we are representing, what our movement is truly about. Fundamentally, we are fighting for a cause on three fronts. An economic, political and social movement. Principally a social movement, that is at least the phase we have now, where social justice, in essence, a culture of selflessness to fight selfishness (the philosophy of oneness as I call it), where a progressive movement seeking leadership or organization is formed as disciplined campers, in particular in the north, especially during the winter, stick it out as the "symbolic" camps, and the larger camp like here in New Haven, continue to resist the system as a base of operations for the movement in general.

Subconsciously the old norms of society that we grew up with, the old prejudices, persistently causing regress as we strive for a new thinking, as they are still there, which has caused to an extent the division we see in the movement now as we are persecuted and many of our camps are shut-down by the State on orders of the 1 percent (elite). We must above all fight ourselves, the pressures and tendencies to act in the old fashion, but that does not mean to do "autonomous action" against each other in that fight, direct action, whether by horizontal democracy, a GA (General Assembly) must be done mainly against the system, not just attacking aggressively its symptoms, but to get to the root cause of the matter and to cure it in the struggle, the cancer of State Capitalism or Corportatism as we know it and all its fascistic policies. And we must know this is about the "we" that this cause is bigger than ourselves, for the cause to prevail we must act as one big family, a collective or community to be formed towards a new society. We must counter the culture or subculture with a counter culture, one with the ideals of love, humanity, equality, solidarity, etc.

Here comes the second front, as there is no order to it, everyone has their role in setting up a revolution, whether a vanguard diehard ready to be arrested like myself, or one who will act as journalist as well, and cover the events or acts the movement carries out. This second front is the economic war. There is a class war chiefly against the working class, poor or homeless class, not to be confused with the middle class (bourgeois). The old thinking of being rich is good, exploitation is ok, will get us nowhere. Imperialism is a system of economic war, battles are fought, but a "hot" war is not to the

31

extent of the Bush era, we have "interventions" for "humanitarian purposes" such as the genocide in Libya on orders from Obama and his pawns in NATO, Obama too has his orders.

The third front is the political one. I may not be very popular in the movement for saying this now, but we must eventually organize a third party to represent the interest of the workers of this country directly, to have the means of production, and to have a more democratic and equal society based on the principles of justice. I do not like to call the current system in the US a 2 party system, it is essentially a one party system with two factions. Both have long been corrupted and bought off by corporations selected as celebrities to play a game of this or that candidate with general disinterest from the average American, as Americans look upon these events with amusement, but not much more. The differences between the two parties are minor, we need an alternative, one that will fight on these three fronts that occupy can provide. Some may block this idea, some may leave the movement as a result, but let them start their own movement, occupy will not be co-opted by either party and must eventually start its own party, I do not think this contradicts Anarchism, I am an Anarcho Socialist and believe both philosophies can be balanced out and bring about true democracy.

To conclude, the paranoia and division which is persistent in the movement shall cease when we have better dialogue and transparency among ourselves in the movement, then we can focus on outreach in the community and recruit new allies and groups to our cause who may differ on methods, but that can continue in a united front with us towards the common ideals we seek as we fight the common enemy, of capital, who's greed has no limit and who represents a small elite we outnumber and will soon conquer in-spite of them having the guns and money, the masses will eventually mobilize the conditions will be made for a revolutionary scenario, the question is when not if, and in this industrialized society of the US, nearing towards a Orwellian nightmare, we can counter it with the counter culture for a better future for our children before it is too late."

That paranoia came in the form of a civil war that was to ensue on camp days after this article was written, which is not to say this article inspired that, I was for unity, which is where the next chapter leaves us.

Chapter 14 In NY For 6 Month Anniversary of Occupy

This chapter is particularly painful to write, not only because this time I was in NY I was having a hard time in the movement, but the level of brutality I witnessed by police, worse than ever, it has been so painful that in the original two versions of my book I did not mention it.

Ty, his wife, and kids, all drove to Brooklyn from New Haven, Ty had his kids were dropped off with a babysitter, and from there, the three of us (Sarah, Ty and I) drove to Zuccotti park. This was March 17th 2012. We arrived near the park with a march in progress, I saw someone I recognized, said hi to him, and I saw him run off and immediately alert Elizabeth Holmes to my presence, I was prepared for

32

confrontation with other occupiers. We got to the park and there was a large group of people already congregating on the park, adding the marchers, we had a few thousand. Ty and I ran into Yoni, who had let me stay in his home 6 months prior. You could see his attitude with me changed. Elizabeth showed up and yelled to Yoni "Al is here!", I turned around, with Ty by my side, and yelled at Elizabeth, I told her I knew Yoni, that he was in New Haven with me, that I was in his home, she then ran off, she did not realize I was right there.

I later found a Dominican man who was a member of the military arrested the last time I was in NY, he said this time if the cops tried to arrest him he would outrun them, he made the salute, refused to move from the wall where we were earlier, and when they tried to grab him he ran, it was impressive how fast he was, if he only walked off he would not be arrested, I later found out they were able to put him in the patty-wagon.

All of a sudden I was talking with a girl about a poll they were doing on police behavior, and a lot of people were all running in one direction. I of course followed them to see what the commotion was about, this was down the street from the park. To my shock a 16 year old girl was being beaten by police. This is not to be confused with the young girl who was going into a seizure later, and was refused medical attention for hours. This 16 year old I don't even think was a occupier, she was used to get people out of the park so the cops could take it over, which was done in broad daylight.

Ty witnessed later the taking of a clearly marked medic by police, where his head was thrown through a glass wall. I was very lucky that night. We tried to do a de-arrest to stop the police beating her and detaining her, opening her blouse and desperately trying to provoke us to violence, but to no avail. Later that day I met up with J Lo and we attended General Assembly at the park. Finally the cops came en masse to shut the park down, I locked arms with others, but was in the line behind, and somehow we got broken up and in the confusion was able to get out. I then attended the march to occupy Union Square, a tactical retreat. Ty was there waiting for me. And then exhausted I was able to talk to the crowd. I made a call to defend the last major camp in New England, for people to come to defend camp in New Haven! In-spite of all my problems with the movement, I used the last energy in me to defend it. Ty and Sarah went back to Brooklyn, and left me at Union Square to rest with my comrades on what blankets we could find, with the few that were not arrested and willing to be the first to occupy Union Square, the next morning we returned to New Haven, and I heard they held on to Union Square a few more days, which was about a hour march from Wall Street.

Upon arriving in New Haven, I spoke at General Assembly saying I witnessed a civil war in NY, with brutality of the police like I never seen, ironically New Haven soon after was to have a civil war of their own, but among ourselves...

Chapter 15 New Haven Civil War

Am known for being an ironic person, so I start this chapter with an image when we were all united. You can see Cassie there, and Don in the blue shirt in front of me. As I worked with the legal team I got the text that said we won an injunction to keep the camp open as we appealed the court's decision to shut down our camp thanks to the efforts of Norm Pattis, our lawyer, a respected attorney from the area. I was the one who collected the names that would form the 8 plaintiffs to keep our camp open, who included Josh, Danielle, Ty, and Don. It is sad how it all fell apart. Similar to what happened in Boston. The civil war was not just based on ideological differences, and racism was not involved so much like in Tampa. There was no such tension as virtually everyone in New Haven camp was white. It

was an inevitable struggle essentially between the homeless occupiers and non-homeless occupiers, although some did not make that distinction. It started when after the barricade was made separating one part of the camp from the other to stop a "raiding" of the camp from the cops, but was actually used to separate one group of occupiers from another. Danielle when she defended our camp in court said the ones on the other side were not real occupiers. And when asked about the woman who was sexually assaulted by a level 3 sex offender on the other side of the barricade on camp, said she was homeless, not a occupier. I was attacked for defending this woman, for standing up to the bullies on camp who owned the tents of the homeless occupiers, occupiers in their own right. My tent was eventually thrown in the dumpster with all my things when I came back to camp, but then people finally came to defend me and let me stay a few more days before I could get to Boston again, in fact I came back to New Haven before this happened at the assurance of Ty, my ally, who I thought had everyone at General Assembly agree I could come back, but in fact the aggression against me only continued, as it had against other homeless occupiers, I remember one morning in those hard days waking up and seeing my late sister sleeping beside me, she was always with me.

I admit at the risk of incriminating myself I did have relations with a girl on camp in New Haven, one time, a traveler who told me she wanted to have all the guys she could under her belt on camp, one night stands, I thought she was joking but later realized she was serious. People found out and kept coming up to her and telling her rumors from Boston, but I don't think she ever accused me of anything. Out of respect for her privacy I won't mention her name. Here is an article I wrote at the time which touches on the ideological differences in particular on the question of leadership, then an article I wrote just before returning to Tampa which defends the homeless occupiers.

How The Anti-Leader Mentality Is Destroying Our Movement (Perspective From An Occupier)

March 22, 2012 at 1:41pm

Our movement is being destroyed from within by many forces, one of the principal forces in this struggle to maintain and expand a movement, (the latter seems almost an impossibility at this point in occupy) is the anti-leader mentality, the total discouragement, in particular, of leadership or any type of discipline, organization, or militancy, which is essential to the survival and progress of any movement for social change, whether political or economic justice, as history has shown. Some forms of Anarchism, especially in the US, are all-out against leadership they see it as anti-horizontal and anti-egalitarian. Power must be taken from the corporations, we are all in agreement they have too much power, the question is how, like any Anarchist I believe power must be taken from the bottom up, not the top down, this is the firm belief and principle of many a revolutionary and activist in our movement.

If we changed our path to destruction now, and instead, encouraged leaders, exceptional people (not the contradictory statement we are all leaders which is laughable) we could progress. I was manipulated in the movement to believe the contradiction, that we are leaderless and leaderfull, now I see, leaders, as they have always been, true leaders, see leaders in others, those who lead the charge at the marches and protests. Those who speak in public and motivate people into action. The notion we are all leaders is nice but void of any reality and has no use in this movement anymore, many other activists who have discussed this with me agree with that as well. We must form our own political party to hope to make any political change in this country.

Most occupiers agree we can't rely on the "2 party system" or as I call it, the 1 party system with two factions, but they don't want to talk about solutions, such as making our own party and trying to work within the system of laws to use against the very system that oppresses us, like when I encouraged lawyers in New Haven to get an injunction on the camp so it would not be shut-down, I was criticized for these efforts, even after they worked, as the camp is still there. This is because of the mentality of "do nothing but chores, and attend a protest, but don't be outspoken, don't dare be a leader or want to be a leader, we are all equal." There comes a time when utterly ridiculous statements like this need to be pointed out for their hypocrisy. They are essentially killing the movement, as the brute mentality of destruction of property rather than boycotting the proprietors is destroying the movement and the elephant is being ignored, the real problems internally.

When Saladin asked a Crusader what Jerusalem meant to him, he said nothing, and everything. These are the contradictions we live in. When a camp is shutdown, and I been through four raids, then we are told a new camp means nothing, a leader means nothing, etc, when all these things can mean everything to a lot of people. White middle class kids who have no experience of poverty or homelessness are at the forefront of destroying property in the name of Anarchy and Occupy destroying what little good image we have in the public. Through intimidation, of other occupiers, and the police, they continue to bring us to regress.

35

Nevertheless, I am in favor of self-defense, I witnessed brutality like never before in New York recently. At the same time I know we must maintain the moral high-ground, or as some call it, moral authority, but as soon as you tell an Anarchist authority, like when you tell some Feminists girl to a 14 year old, they go hysterical. The 14 year old must be a woman! It used to be spelt only womyn to a Feminist in plural form like during the 1970s. Look not all authority is bad, we are taught to respect authority as inherent, and this is wrong, but that does not mean we can be democratic, equal, and horizontal, and accept authority exists, the GA (General Assembly of Occupy) acts as a body or legislation of authority or as bureaucrats. Some black Anarchists call it an evil needed, but that is the same justification for voting Democrat or Republican. Like the lesser evil. GA is not evil. It is a reflection of a flawed system fighting another flawed system and we need constructive criticism to reform our system from within so that we can bring about a peaceful revolution in this country once and for all, and let this influence other nations fighting exploitation whether by Capitalist groups or Corporations. Towards a new society, a new era!

Why Homeless Occupiers Are The Best Occupiers

April 6, 2012 at 2:32pm

It's no secret I been homeless the past 6 months and I am not ashamed to say this, homeless occupiers are the best occupiers since they have nothing to lose, they are many of those on the frontlines willing to get arrested for the movement, I almost got canned countless times but the two times I was arrested for the movement was on my own terms. I have been through 5 raids, 1 of which I was arrested at, in my native Boston. Occupy is going through a divisive phase unfortunately, where the homeless are convenient scapegoats, I been to New York three times to address the housing crisis, I offered these homeless people my part of camp in New Haven, I say mine, as the rest of camp I was non grata for speaking out for the homeless, one of which was sexually assaulted.

Her assault was brushed off as "Oh she was homeless, so she is not an occupier." Even if she was not a occupier (which she was) she is a human being and our security should have protected her, she was on our camp! When camps are shutdown they can go to a warm home to see Mommy & Daddy but us homeless have to go back on the streets and go to a shelter with no security where we can get robbed or assaulted. Violent "Anarchists" love to bully on homeless people in the name of occupy, instead of going after cops, they make "autonomous action" against campers or occupiers kicking them out or putting them in another part of camp.

36

The excuse much of the time is "people are uncomfortable with their drinking or drug use", when most of the people on the camp drink or use drugs there. The media has ignored the countless articles and parts of interviews by homeless occupiers or those who support them that make clear on the existence of homeless occupiers, but this is ignored, I stress they not only exist, they are in most cases, the best of occupiers, and this injustice cannot go on much longer. Soon on the remaining camps the homeless will have to make an army to defend themselves with sticks, I am for non-violence but I believe in self-defense. The shunning, not giving of food, or attacks, on the homeless, must end, occupy needs direction, there needs to be a way out of this mess and mob rule will not solve our problems, we need tough love, the truth to be said and for us to do something about it once and for all.

Chapter 16 Return To Tampa

It is necessary in this chapter to show two speeches I gave. But first I will show my reaction to the camp in New Haven being shut down when I was in Tampa, just a couple weeks after being voted out of West Tampa, when I was still in shock for everything that happened. I will explain however the context of the first speech that proceeds the reaction, that one in regards to Tampa. A petition from local businesses in West Tampa, where the Occupy Tampa camp had been located since January 2012, to kick the occupiers out, was made, this was in July 2012. The first speech I gave to city council, considering my role in the movement, it was very ironic.

My Reaction To The Eviction of Occupy New Haven
April 21, 2012 at 10:59am

Many of you know my connection to ONH as being a problematic one, but I still feel in my heart a sadness for the loss of this camp, I had good experiences on that camp. I arrived on camp the hero from Boston, the man who was arrested at Dewey's last stand. The day after arriving I was arrested with 7 others on the day of action February 29th in front of one of the most corrupt corporations of this nation. Anyone who had doubts about me at that point then went away. I was applauded for being arrested a

second time for the movement. I came out in the paper saying what an honor it was to be part of the last major camp in New England.

I made friends with our lawyers and became the contact for legal info, I got plaintiff's names on a list to ask for an injunction, and announced the injunction to a applauding crowd, and helped lead the march to City Hall to demand the mayor speak to us, and I got to embarrass him with my question on the proprietors, if they were constitutional with their rule over the Green where the camp is.

37

Camaraderie with half of those 7 arrested with me, who lived on camp with me, was strong. The others came mostly from Hartford and visited our camp from time to time or I ran into them at protests in different towns. But soon after arriving in New Haven, rumors from Boston spread to camp. Immediately a campaign to have me removed from camp ensued which initially started behind my back. I did all I could to stay.

By the end of March it was clear my status on camp was not what it was when I first came to camp. So I went to Boston a couple days to try to deal with my problems and came back thinking things would settle over. By the beginning of April I left camp never to come back. I left with a broken heart but no hate towards the camp, in fact I made a strong condemnation against "J Lo" someone I had a temporary alliance with on camp, when she called the Fire Marshall behind my back bringing down the barricade built on camp. I was not for the barricade being up all the time, but that is something the camp should have decided without city intervention. I want to send my solidarity and a personal greeting to my allies left in New Haven, and even extended my sorrow for those who consider themselves my enemies.

Speech In Favor of Petition Against West Tampa Camp

July 19, 2012 at 12:05pm

"Corporately owned West Tampa camp, a camp owned by a man who has made himself rich off the exploitation of women, is racist and discriminatory towards those who dare to believe in God. Am I talking third party, speculating? No! This has happened to myself and countless others unjustly forced out of camp, which has turned into a cult of personality of atheist impositionists, violent anarchists, & sexist anti-male elements, with the occasional vandalism, drug use, orgy and robbery for the few who remain. There are no real activists left who spend a night there. When the witch-trial, aka General Assembly happened against me, back in April this year on camp, mind you this is the first time I have talked publicly about this, this is not a vendetta but justice, I was discouraged from speaking Spanish to Marisol, before it started, Marisol a widow who like me, has been arrested doing non-violent civil disobedience, I was the only one to show up to support her in court, but I was too late, her poor English was taken advantage of and she signed a deal which makes her pay monthly fees while she is a mother living on a pension. When I confronted the legal team about this later, they did not seem to care, if she becomes homeless as a result of this, so what? Marisol, like me had her cell stolen from camp, and later when she was in New York had her tent and valuable documents taken, no doubt she has enemies on camp as she is my friend.

During the inquisition against me on camp, I was told I only had intervals of 2 minutes to defend myself, I was told City Council also gives two minutes, is this not the system they are fighting? In a court of law I would have more time. Lincoln would be ashamed. I was the first to be kicked out under so called safe spaces policy. I was asked during the General Assembly to swear to God the ridiculous

38

rumors against me were not true, I did, and Joel, one of my accusers, a known anti-Christian said swearing to deities is irrelevant. He later perjured himself in court documents against a friend of mine. I respect atheism but they burned the sign that said in God we trust, they have a sign that says We Aint Going Nowhere which mocks the community and local businesses. When Redner, the owner of the camp, was informed of the discrimination he said it was not a credible complaint even when whites who were kicked out were let back in to camp. This is not a free speech issue. They ask me where is solidarity, I ask them where is solidarity. The revolution must adapt from camps. We know what JFK said about revolution. Not just the State and its agents promote violence, elements of black bloc in the movement as well. They ask me why I am an activist, before the death of my sister I was an activist, and now I fight for the future of her daughter, there is no greater cause to me. It gives me no satisfaction to expose my former comrades, I do so with a broken heart, but we must speak the truth, even if the petition is not passed occupy knows what's the right thing to do. Vindication for all those kicked out unjustly."

Here is the second speech given a month later after Redner, the owner of the camp, said they had to leave by September, after the RNC, and after I kicked Tommy Parisi from my home, an enemy of occupy who took advantage of my differences with them and accompanied me to the first city council meeting against them and gave his own speech:

Speech In Defense of Occupy At City Council of Tampa

August 16, 2012 at 12:24pm

"I believe Redner's eviction notice for September 15th is a maneuver to make sure the camp can be there for RNC. Nevertheless, for the sake of unity, and for solidarity for the original occupy as I took part in civil disobedience to defend camps through-out the nation, in-spite of being for adaptation, and against the excesses of Occupy lately, I hereby retract my position, and wholeheartedly wish Occupy good luck on being one of the last remaining camps in the nation. I hope non-violent activists can come and Occupy can learn from her mistakes. She has made no attempt to reconcile with me, on the contrary, however out of my own logic I have come to this conclusion.

In the final analysis, history will be the judge of us all, let us be for understanding and love, rather than hate and division. We must respect each other and our rights, learn from our faults, and then progress can come, dignity can be restored, this I have learned from my father and my experiences, I shall not forget..."

No one spoke against occupy that day, Tommy did not show up, he was probably back living with his mother outside of Tampa. I expected some conciliatory moves from occupy, or at the very least for them to back off their attacks on me. Quite the contrary during the Republican National Convention soon after that they printed out letters against me warning activists to stay away from me, that I was a sexual predator, that I wanted to set people up for the FBI in my "safehouse", that I was with Tommy, even though they already knew I disassociated from him. I had activists stay in my home still, activists who knew me, I still went to a protest here or there, including in my neighborhood Ybor City, I

39

marched with my comrades, in-spite of some from other areas sent there to call me a rapist. I would suite them but this would cause division. Mitch Perry of CL Tampa paper quoted me as calling occupy racist in July but did another article in August where he failed to mention my extending of the olive branch, which I find dishonest on his part as a journalist. This book is to finally show my side.

Conclusion

I became one of the 8 plaintiffs to keep the last major camp open in New England, New Haven, CT, I was arrested in that state for the second time in the movement (http://www.theday.com/article/20120229/NWS01/120229563/Eight-arrested-when-Occupy-movement-comes-to-Pfizer), but there was a civil war on that camp which some details I left out I may put in later on, such as how toxic waste from the hospital was put in my tent causing me a fever, but my strength and the will to see my niece made me recover fast, and it made me stronger, I refused to be intimidated, even when I was told 30 men were going to be sent to kick me out, who never came, as I held my stick and was willing to fight on till the end, and smoked the small cheap cigars to calm down. New Haven where Ty finally took me in again, my last day there.

In Tampa they had plotted against me to be kicked out of the movement as well which I allude to in the city council speeches, the second speech helped keep the West Tampa camp open, which was the final decision. I ended up taking part in protests during the Republican National Convention in Tampa in August 2012 in-spite of all of this (http://www.tampabay.com/news/politics/elections/many-republican-national-convention-protesters-wont-follow-tampas-script/1236722) and attended since then protests

40

and gone to Boston and reconciled with many comrades. Carlos Arredondo who I mention in one of my chapters has turned into a national hero for his role in saving lives in the Boston Marathon bombings, he is known as the "man in the cowboy hat" who saved Jeff Bauman, who revealed one of the identities of the terrorists who planted the bombs, as Carlos was volunteering with his wife Melida for the Red Cross and his son Alex, who was a soldier, was honored at the event, I need not provide a reference for that. It was nice to get back in touch with him and interview him.

I plan to get into more detail my participation towards the end of the movement in a second edition in this book or in a later article. I hope this book can bring clarity to my role in the movement and we can learn from this experience. It is not to manipulate or play the victim but simply show my experience, my truth, for history. Sometimes being right too early can cause you problems, make you enemies, especially when you let people know openly, transparently, but I was wrong many times too, and had made mistakes, we all do, let this be a testament to the collective experience, and not just the individual experience.

Description of additional photos in their order:

The arrest at the Pfizer corporation, where I started the chant "Bring out a rep!" as they refused to do so.

In NYC New Years with James, Nunes and others of the Boston crowd.

Ocupemos el barrio rally (Spanish occupy).

Mugshots on front page of Boston Herald after our arrest at Occupy Boston.

In a General Assembly meeting sitting near Elizabeth Holmes (in orange).

By my tent I named after my sister upon my arrival in Tampa.

In a People of Color Working Group meeting in Boston.

With fellow 46er Brandon, and others, after Martin Luther King day event in Boston.

Reunited with Richard Knight on camp in Boston.

With Noam Chomsky in his office.

At the wall the site of the General Assemblies on camp in Boston.

You can still see our smiles in-spite of the fogginess, this is when I sat down and said lets lock arms guys, and we stayed till the end, till we were finally arrested defending camp in Boston.

The arrival of Jose, fellow 46er, in New Haven.

41

FACES OF OCCUPY
EAGAN: THEY'RE PATRIOTS / CARR: THEY'RE IDIOTS